BUSES
YEARBOOK 2004

We're all over London

THE BIG
BUS
COMPANY

B'S SIGHTSEEING TOUR OF LONDON

SIGHTSEEING

THE ORIGINAL
BIG BUS

TOUR

A624 THV

Edited by STEWART J. BROWN

Ian Allan
PUBLISHING

BUSES
YEARBOOK 2004

Contents

First published 2003

ISBN 0 7110 2938 5

Published by Ian Allan Publishing

an imprint of Ian Allan Publishing Ltd, Hersham, Surrey KT12 4RG. Printed by Ian Allan Printing Ltd, Hersham, Surrey KT12 4RG.

Code: 0308/E2

Front cover: **FirstGroup bought long-wheelbase Volvo Olympians for some of its fleets. This is a First Edinburgh vehicle, new in 1998 with Alexander Royale body, in Princes Street, Edinburgh.** *Gavin Booth*

Back cover: **Rossendale's fleet of Dennis Darts includes some with Plaxton bodies. These are 40-seat 11.3m-long Super Pointer Darts. There were 14 in operation by 2000.** *W. M. Ewing*

Title page: **A Big Bus Company Titan passes one of Britain's tourist icons in Parliament Square, London. Ex-London Titans have been replacing ex-London Fleetlines in the Big Bus Company fleet.** *Stewart J. Brown*

WHAT'S IN A NAME?

Manufacturers often pick strange names for their products. *David Thrower* takes a look at the familiar and the less familiar names used by bus and coach makers.

What do the Gnu, the Cheetah, the Wolf and the Lion have in common? Does a Condor fly faster than a Falcon? Can a Pelican even fly at all? And precisely what's the difference between a Merlin and a Swift? Are they both migratory? They certainly both catch fire.

Do you know which is the most warlike — the Invader, the Crusader, the Victor, the Avenger or the Valiant? Perhaps bus wars are older than we realise, after all? And after the battle, does the vanquished sue for peace by shouting "Pax!"?

Which can travel the furthest — an Arrow, a Javelin or a Dart? Does a Valkyrie or a Centaur, or for that matter a Titan, appear from out of a Nimbus, or even ride on one? And are they accompanied as they cross the heavens by Lightning, or Comets?

Do bullfighters sometimes shout "OLAZ!" in error?

Which is the lower, a Lowlander or a Lowloader? And which is the more competitive, a Marathon or an Olympic? Can a Metropolitan be used in rural areas? And did Scout ever operate Cubs? Would Badgerline have purchased a fleet of Badgers, had it operated in the 1930s?

These arcane questions might fox (but not Vixen) a contender (no, not a Commer Contender) on one of those mind-numbing quiz programmes that seem to have replaced quality television productions these days. But, of course, they are all terms that are familiar to us bus enthusiasts. And they do beg the question: just why is a type of bus or coach given a particular name?

Bus and coach names down the years have

At a time when few buses carried model names, the Leyland Comet was an exception. Note the Comet badge on the side of the bonnet on this 1949 Douglas Corporation bus with Park Royal bodywork. Most Comet chassis were bodied as trucks; buses and coaches were rare. *Alan Broughall*

Thornycroft had unusual names for its chassis. This was a Nippy. Purchased new by MacBrayne's of Glasgow in 1950, it is seen in 1966 running for McLachlan's of Tayvallich. Bodywork was by Croft of Glasgow. *Stewart J. Brown*

covered much of the world's wildlife, some of mythology's gods, a few of humanity's races and much else besides. They have also encapsulated some other more obscure genres of terminology — PSUC, for example, or the aforementioned OLAZ. And just a few have gone on to form public transport's very own contribution to the English language — Lodekka, Loline, Routemaster. The last-mentioned, perhaps uniquely, is now well known by the general public.

The practice of giving a name to a model has been applied, though perhaps not with the same degree of enthusiasm, to designs of both chassis and bodywork. But mostly, the chassis has taken precedence. For instance, you can have half a dozen different Dennis Darts, but they are all just 'Darts', and their differing bodywork by Plaxton, Carlyle or whoever goes largely unmentioned.

Early days

As with much transport history, it is difficult to be sure quite where the practice of giving a bus type a name actually started. Horse-drawn vehicles had sorted themselves into various sub-types at an early stage. At first, these frequently merely described the layout. For example, there was the 1850s 'knifeboard', with its upstairs longitudinal seating resembling a Victorian knifeboard, and the 'garden seat' omnibus, with the seating provided by small crossways seats. The term 'charabanc' was in use by the 1890s.

Some of the vehicles of the early horse era were simply described by the number of horses required to pull them. Then the terms began to be mixed together, so you had a 'two-horse charabanc', and

everyone would know roughly what this meant. It hardly mattered who had constructed it. All these vehicles would be assembled locally, with every large town having a number of bodybuilding workshops and wheelwrights, so there was little need for sales brochures, and no necessity to give each product a name. Vehicle construction was open to anyone with joinery skills and a supply of timber.

Even in early motorbus days little changed, because there were dozens of manufacturers, each producing an extremely limited range, with sometimes just one type in production. These were the days of long-lost manufacturers such as Arrol-Johnston, Gloster and Straker-Squire. Then, as technology advanced, so the names of inventors or manufacturers (sometimes one and the same person) became well known. Thus we began to see models such as the Clarkson steamer, although, as this design developed, specific model names were used by the company, such as the Chelmsford, reflecting its place of construction.

Where novel propulsion was used, this might be incorporated into the name of the product, hence the 'Electrobus' — an early example of a catchy name that still sounds good a century later. But many vehicles were still simply termed by their maker's name and engine size, for instance the Armstrong-Whitworth 32hp, or the De Dion-Bouton 24hp.

As manufacturing became more organised so the classic companies began to emerge. These used printed sales publicity, because their products needed to be promoted by more than just word of mouth, and so the use of model/type names became more the norm. Hence we had the Leyland SG and Maudslay ML types of the early 1920s. Other companies started using names rather than letters. For example, a company called Moss & Wood imported a Swiss-built motorbus chassis which was sold under the name 'Orion', a term that was to become much more famous when used the second time around, half a century later.

Over the years, some very odd names indeed were chosen. As long ago as 1833, an experimental steam bus bore the name 'Autopsy', which well might actually have been prophetic in the days when safety valves were weighted down to produce more speed. A particularly far-sighted name was given by Dennis to its 1913 Olympia Show model, the Dennis Subsidy. Another odd choice was the 1920s Reo Speedwagon, with its name redolent of reckless driving. And the imported Dodge Fargo of the late 1920s summons up visions of being headed off at the pass, or of passengers leaping aboard from galloping horses racing alongside.

And then there was the Titanic. The Leyland Titanic was launched well after the ship of the same name achieved infamy. Why did the company not choose the *Carpathia* or the *Mauretania*? In fact, RMS *Titanic*'s sister ship was the *Olympic*, and ironically this too eventually turned up, after a fashion (it was probably the 1948 Games that Leyland really had in mind) for the single-decker design of the 1950s. Another curious choice was the Tilling-Stevens Successor of the late 1930s, begging the question 'Successor to what?'. No operators ever ran any, so it wasn't actually a success …

The Zoo

The animal and bird world has provided much inspiration for manufacturers looking for a name for their latest product.

Undoubtedly the greatest use of this was by Leyland, and the range was sometimes known by commentators as the 'Leyland Zoo'. We have seen most of the big cats covered, plus some other species. The big cats combined an image of snarling power with speed. Leyland seems to have started with the king of beasts, the Lion, which it brought out in 1925. This was followed by the Lioness in the same year and the Tiger in 1927, with the Cheetah padding stealthily along behind in 1935. Their man-eating and mauling characteristics seem to have been studiously ignored, and this is in some ways curious. After all, we would never have seen the Leyland Shark, would we? Perhaps in belated recognition that these animals might convey an image that was not entirely benevolent,

Leyland brought in some other, less threatening species. So, from 1932, we had the various Cubs, far more cuddly and less likely to eat their passengers at bus stops. Obviously, this too had its limitations, and so we eventually had the Badger and the Panda too. Interestingly, other, non-animal naming systems were also used by Leyland during this period, as described elsewhere, and we were thus ultimately spared some of the more obscure cat species.

Leyland's animals made a big comeback after World War 2. This highlights a problem: when a name has become successful, there is great temptation to reuse it. This could be on the basis of success begetting success, or it might just indicate a lack of imagination. Either way, the 1950s saw the big cats back with a vengeance, with the Royal Tiger and Tiger Cub, to be pursued by the spotless Leopard and, less sure-footedly, the Panther and its even more unsteady Panther Cub.

Despite Leyland's very early pre-emptive safari, we also saw the occasional use of animals by others, for instance the Albion Clydesdale.

Some animals would have been a complete non-starter, for obvious reasons. A Leyland Skunk could never have sold, even if it had carried 120 passengers in extreme comfort at 25mpg fuel consumption. The Thornycroft Tortoise or the Crossley Crab would have fared no better than the

Tiger Cubs were cuddly creatures, and surely few were cuter than a one-off batch supplied to Alexander (Midland) in 1961. They had 38-seat Alexander bodies. The coach behind is an altogether fiercer Royal Tiger, also bodied by Alexander.
Stewart J. Brown

Morris Millipede or the Sentinel Sloth, though the name Millipede might well have been very useful for London's experimental four-axle XRM design of the late 1970s.

But some decidedly peculiar beasts have occasionally escaped onto the streets, for example the Leyland Gnu (which really was peculiar, having most of its wheels at the front) and the Beaver, which is often an unwelcome mammal in its native habitat. A great opportunity was also missed by not naming a deregulation-era minibus design the Lemming, or even the Locust.

Birds have been less common, and sometimes, when they have been used, the results have not

Top: **Somebody at Burlingham must surely have been joking in calling this body the Gannet. The logic behind naming a coach after a bird best known for its enormous appetite was that its predecessor had been the Seagull. Paterson of Dalry operated this Gannet, on a Ford Thames chassis.** *Harry Hay*

Above: **Swift was a name used by AEC in the 1960s and then again by Leyland in the 1980s. The Leyland Swift was a light mid-engined bus. This example, operated by Stevensons of Uttoxeter, has Reeve Burgess Harrier bodywork.** *Stewart J. Brown*

been happy, such as the Merlin and Swift. And more than a few blunderbuses might well have been more appropriately launched under the name Albatross.

Royalty and gods

Royalty has gifted a number of names to buses and coaches. This is scarcely appropriate, given that they don't travel on them. Most famous of all the royal names have been the Regent and the Regal.

Some other names that were presumably meant to convey confidence in authority have succeeded in going right over the top. Even in the 1930s, during the rise of Fascism, some very doubtful names were being bestowed, the most glaringly inappropriate being Morris-Commercial's Dictator, plus its Imperial, though its Leader was less oppressive. Quite recently, we have also seen the Setra Imperial. Democracy has still to become fashionable, apparently.

Stepping up to the gods, these too have had some successes, most notably Titan, mythical child of Uranus and Gaea, and patron of large diesel engines. Leyland's first use of this term lasted from the late 1920s until 1969 — surely an all-time record

Above: **There were Regents in production at AEC for over 40 years. This is a Mk III model of 1949 with Weymann body, running for Aberdeen Corporation in 1965.** *Stewart J. Brown*

Below: **A stylish script badge on the radiator tells those who are interested that this AEC is a Regal. It is a 1950 Mk III with Weymann body, operated by Devon General.** *Alan Broughall*

Below: **The mightiest bus of them all? There were few places in Britain where you couldn't see a Titan in operation in the 1950s and 1960s – a bit like the Dennis Dart of today. This classic Titan is a 1946 PD1 operated by Darwen Corporation.** *Stewart J. Brown collection*

— followed rapidly by a second-generation Titan from the late 1970s. This raises a related point. The name 'Titan' did not always see common use amongst ordinary busmen out on the streets. For instance, in the days when Greater Manchester Transport still had a large number of such vehicles, these were invariably referred to as 'PDs'. When asked, staff would have not the slightest idea what these two letters actually stood for, but it is interesting that the alphanumeric 'PD2' was far better understood than the sales term 'Titan'. Equally curiously, the second-time-around Titan of the 1970s and 1980s was invariably termed just that — Titan — despite selling in much smaller numbers.

Nations and Nationals

Use has only very occasionally been made of nations to give a design a name. The example that will spring to mind in readers aged over 40 will be the Guy Arab, running as it did to Mk V and operating on the streets from the 1930s to the 1980s. Presumably the term owed something to the

legendary Arab steed rather than to the residents of Saudi Arabia. This, if true, was ironic, because the Guy Arab's qualities were best summed up as slogging, hard-wearing reliability rather than dashing speed.

Perhaps one of the most successful terms of all time was the National. This was undoubtedly due to the highly-standardised range and its wide customer base.

Regional or urban names (rather than true nation-states) have fared quite well. We have had the Albion Aberdonian, sales of which certainly weren't

Right: **For over 30 years most Guy buses were Arabs, even if the only thing the first model shared with the last was its name. This is a 1947 example, with Roberts body, operated by Burton-upon-Trent Corporation.** *Alan Broughall*

Below: **Most Seddon buses were Pennines of one sort or another, taking their name from the hills near the company's Oldham factory. Blackburn Corporation operated this 1972 Pennine RU with East Lancs body.** *Stewart J. Brown*

Above: **The Atlantean was one of Britain's most common buses throughout the 1970s and well into the 1980s. Merseyside Transport was a late user of the type, taking its last, with Alexander bodies, in 1984.** *Stewart J. Brown*

Right: **Albion used a range of 'V' names over a long period. The Venturer was a double-deck chassis. Cheltenham District Traction ran this Metro-Cammell-bodied bus, new in 1949.** *R. F. Mack*

confined to the Grampians. Less happy was the Guy Wulfrunian, named after the queen Wulfreda. Perhaps its undoing was in trying to operate outside (or, for that matter, inside) the boundary of Wolverhampton. And in the very early days we had the Lothian.

Some more recent names have been localised, for example Wadham Stringer's Portsdown body, named after a hill north of Portsmouth. We have also had the 1930s Crossley Mancunian, which can hardly have engendered enthusiasm in nearby Liverpool. In the mid-1960s the Mancunian name re-surfaced, applied to a superb design with distinctively-styled bodywork and very deep front windows, carried on Leyland or Daimler chassis.

Some names were a good attempt that just didn't quite come off. An example is the Daimler Freeline, which was neither free to operate nor to travel on, and the Roadliner, which suffered its own set of problems. Even Daimler's most famous product, the Fleetline, had a name that didn't actually mean anything.

There are also a few puzzles and potential pitfalls. To the uninformed the Atlantean implied a resident of Atlantis, a fabled land now lost beneath the waves of the Atlantic Ocean. But it actually meant 'resembling the giant Atlas'. If you look, the badge has an image of a god holding up the weight of the world on his shoulder.

Quite a few names seem to have been chosen solely to echo the first letter of the manufacturer's own name. So we have the Albion Aberdonian, Atkinson Alpha, Crossley Condor, Commer Commando, Dennis Domino, Maudslay Magna and Plaxton Paramount. But this echo effect wasn't always adopted, and, to take one example, Albion fixed upon the letter V, so we had the Viking, Valkyrie, Valiant, Venturer and Victor.

A few names were so similar that they virtually cancelled each other out. Dennis offered both the Ace and the Mace in the 1930s, and one wonders just how many people knew confidently which one was which.

Lodekka was a clever name for a low-height model, being used by Bristol in the 1950s and 1960s for a classic design with an ECW body which achieved a balanced appearance few of its rivals could match. Scottish Omnibuses owned this 1959 bus, seen in Glasgow's George Square. *Harry Hay*

Of course, to incorporate the term 'master', or some such equivalent, is to give a name a certain ring of success, and so we have had a whole string of somethingmasters. Quite apart from London's Routemasters, we have witnessed Leyland's Worldmaster, AEC's Bridgemaster and the Rowe Hillmaster. The Bridgemaster's competitor was the Lodekka, by Bristol, which was yet another approach — that of a non-word that made phonetic sense. Dennis's Loline was another attempt at getting this particular message across, though Albion's Lowlander didn't seem quite right — after all, wasn't it the bridge (rather than the land) that was low?

Gobbledegook

A completely different approach to giving a bus a name was to use a letter code. Hence Daimler's famous CVG6, which stood for **C**ommercial **V**ictory **G**ardner 6-cylinder, the victory in question being the that of the Allies at the end of World War 2 (and Gardner, of course, the engine make). Bristol used a similar system, for example the RELH6G. Although it looked like gobbledegook, it all actually made sense when decoded, being the Bristol RE (**R**ear **E**ngine) type in its **l**onger form with **h**igh floor and a **6**-cylinder **G**ardner engine.

In fact, a surprising percentage of bus designs have become known by their coding rather than any proper name. Most of London's classics have achieved immortality by type codings, for example STL, which bizarrely stood for '**S**hort **T**ype **L**ong'. The RF will always be better known by its letter code than by its Regal IV model name. The early attempt to launch the DMS into public consciousness as the 'Londoner' was an abject failure, and it has remained the DMS ever since.

Sometimes the simplest of codes has become the definitive term for evermore, never more so than in the case of the AEC Q type of the mid-1930s. In this case a monopoly has been established, as there will probably never be another Q.

In the earlier years of the last century, in the 1920s and early 1930s, we had the SOS series. This stood for 'Shires' Own Specification', but to the uninitiated it still sounds like a distress signal.

The Tilling group was another to work its way through its alphabet, its G, J, K and L types in particular springing to mind. The Ks and Ls were so numerous and so famous that Bristol — a make long departed — is likely to have prime claim on these letters for years to come, though the K duplicated the earlier London General K double-decker. Obviously, using more than one letter makes it more likely that a claim on a given code will be permanent, and we will probably only ever have one RM, RE or VR, for example.

Bodywork

It is not certain precisely when body types began to attract names, but the practice probably reached its peak in the 1950s, when numerous bodywork manufacturers competed in a boom market.

Right: The Reeve Burgess Beaver has been the longest-lived of the 'big minibus' generation of bodies, although it is now, of course, a TransBus product. That was still far in the future when this Mercedes-Benz with Beaver body entered service with CentreWest on the Southall Shuttle in 1989. *Stewart J. Brown*

Below: Paladin was the name Northern Counties coined for its single-deck bus bodies in the 1990s. Buyers included Stagecoach, operating this Volvo B10M in Manchester. *Stewart J. Brown*

Bottom: Handy-bus was Wright's first body on the Dennis Dart. Go-Ahead Group was a big user of the type. *Stewart J. Brown*

Just a few names, both of bodies and chassis, have helped to convey logical information about the product. In the early 1950s appeared the AEC/Park Royal Monocoach, publicising its construction details, while Duple's Vista coachwork emphasised the design's large windows. A few tried to convey romance, such as the Yeates Riviera (a name later reused by Reeve Burgess) and Duple Caribbean, or drama, like the Weymann Fanfare. Alexander's Strider has a certain purposefulness and sense of setting-out about it, though aren't you supposed to be relaxing on board, rather than striding? The name was actually an oblique reference to the model's first customer, Yorkshire Rider. Alexander also introduced the Dash, rather more applicable to a bus, though perhaps not one stuck in traffic.

Occasionally, body names have duplicated chassis names, though not always during the same era, so we had the aforementioned Leyland Beaver in the 1930s and then Mercedes minibuses with Reeve Burgess Beaver bodywork in the 1980s.

And a few names are puzzling. Exactly what was it that persuaded Northern Counties to name a bodywork design as the Paladin? The dictionary defines 'paladin' as 'any of the twelve peers of Charlemagne's Court, of whom the Count Palatine was the chief'. Ah, I see the connection now ... And, if that were not enough, Northern Counties went on to offer the Palatine too.

Nicknames

Like any object of familiarity, when familiarity turns to nostalgic endearment, so nicknames become common. Some are unflattering, and we have recently heard of 'Metroboxes' and worse. But most are quite affable. An example that has seen ever-greater use in the past decade, as the type has become a classic, is that of 'Queen Mary', summoning images of an 80,000-ton liner rather than the long-dead monarch herself. And, be it noted, despite their Atlantic-crossing prototype, a Glasgow 'Cunarder' (tram) and a Southdown 'Queen Mary' (bus) have nothing whatever in common.

Salford's batch of Mancunians were sometimes known amongst enthusiasts as 'Salcunians'. In Liverpool, the 33ft-long double-deckers of the early 1970s were nicknamed 'Jumbos'.

Some nicknames have a semi-official ring to them. Greater Manchester's 1970s and 1980s Atlanteans and Fleetlines became widely known as 'Standards', at least in the North West of England, and the name has stuck even after the type's demise. Birmingham's 1950s 'Standards' likewise.

Recent trends

The era of deregulation has brought with it some major changes, though the one has not always been the result of the other. We have low-floor

Citybus is such an obvious name that it is surprising nobody used it sooner. It was Volvo's choice for a mid-engined model developed from the B10M coach chassis. This bus in the Midland Red North fleet started life in 1989 with London & Country. It has a Northern Counties body of a style which from 1992 would be called the Palatine. Stewart J. Brown

Above: **There were Tigers with front-mounted engines in the Leyland zoo from the late 1920s to the early 1950s (and on into the 1960s for export markets), and in 1981 the name was revived for a new mid-engined chassis. Most 1980s Tigers were coaches, but there were buses too, as exemplified by this United vehicle with Alexander (Belfast) body.** *Stewart J. Brown*

Right: **One of the last members of Leyland's zoo was the Lynx. Bristol Omnibus had a fleet of them.** *Stewart J. Brown*

buses and, paradoxically (given their use by the elderly) high-floor coaches. Coaches have become bigger, but quite a few single-deck buses have become shorter and narrower. And small minibuses have come and (largely) gone again.

To sell these new products to operators and the public has required some marketing skill, and finding names has been part of this. For full-size buses, the move towards the low-floor bus and changes in the way language is used have combined to bring us some new-style names. We have the Scania MaxCi, the Optare Spectra and Vecta (can we have a Southern Vectis Vecta?) and PMT's Knype. Some of the more conventional designs perpetuated naming fashions of the past, such as Willowbrook's Warrior, or have opted for the alphanumeric coding once more, such as the Alexander ALX400.

Some names have sought to underpin the place of the bus in city life, hence MCW's Metrobus and Volvo's Citybus, the latter copied by Ikarus but spelt Citibus. The Olympian revived the past glories of Leyland, redolent of historic names such as Atlantean and Olympic. Leyland also unleashed yet more big cats just before deregulation, with the Lynx, the Cub (well, a small cat ...) and the Tiger and Royal Tiger.

Some names, such as the Plaxton Verde, left non-linguists scratching their heads. Was it a French swear-word? Is the Nordic made abroad, or is it exported to Scandinavia? And Plaxton's Pointer shares its name with ... a dog. One to market to Greyhound, perhaps? Meanwhile, the Blue Bird has landed — nothing to do with Alexander but American-built school buses (and not even blue).

In the minibus world, we have had the mouthful of the Iveco Turbo Daily City Nipper — more of an entire sentence than a name — and more classic names such as the Metrorider, plus new 'Euro'-sounding names such as Optare's Alero (not to be confused with Austin's Allegro).

Top: The Olympian started life as a Leyland in 1980 and, for UK operation, ended as a Volvo in 2000. Alexander bodied this Volvo Olympian for Capital Citybus in 1997. *Stewart J. Brown*

Above: Verde (Italian for green) was the name chosen by Plaxton in 1991 for a new city-bus body, seen here on a City of Oxford Volvo B10B. *Stewart J. Brown*

Top right: Images of a high-tech future were no doubt in Duple's mind in 1982, when it christened its new Laser coach body, but

sadly Duple had no future, high-tech or otherwise. This is an example of the short-lived body on a Grey-Green Leyland Tiger. *Stewart J. Brown*

Right: The Falcon name was used more than once by Dennis. The last Falcon was a heavy-duty rear-engined model, usually bodied as a single-deck bus. Mayne of Manchester operated this Falcon with Wadham Stringer Vanguard body from 1991. It had been new to Alder Valley in 1983 and had been rebodied in 1987 following fire damage. *Stewart J. Brown*

Some of the van-derived products brought their parcel-carrying names with them — Transit, Sherpa — but the more refined designs sought to re-establish credibility with names such as Optare's CityPacer. A few of the minibus-associated names also seemed to project the wrong image, bodywork by Dormobile conjuring up a picture of a yawning driver, his passengers all sound asleep and missing their stops. And a Freight Rover Sherpa never sounded right for a passenger service, with visions of passengers being piled in the back amongst the boxes and sacks. And would Friar Tuck have fitted comfortably into a Robin Hood-bodied minibus? A few names were good, Omni, for example, both suggesting 'omnibus' and being one that truly was accessible 'for all'.

For coaches, we had the Skyliner — quite appropriate, given its height — and the Metroliner, intended to convey an image of purposeful comfort. Imports brought new names such as Setra (a contraction of *selbst tragend* — German for integral), whilst companies such as Duple responded with

15

names such as Laser, and Bova introduced its Futura, at least a name that conveys up-to-dateness. The final frontiers of outer space still beckon with LAG's Galaxy, whilst much more terrestrial-sounding is Plaxton's Interurban.

As well as launching new names — like Trident — for its buses, Dennis dusted off past successes such as Falcon and Lance, which (at least for those in the know) hinted at Aldershot & District's green buses pottering along Hampshire lanes. Some animals made an entry for the first (and, hopefully, last) time, such as Berkhof's Elk. If Maudslay were still trading, perhaps we would see the Maudslay Moose, the two models standing nose-to-nose, rear-view mirrors entangled …

Classics

So which names have been most successful? To some extent, this must reflect the numbers sold and their lifespan on the streets, the Routemaster and the Dart coming to mind.

A catchy name certainly helps. Both the RT and the Routemaster sold in four-figure quantities and ran on London's streets for four decades, yet, outside enthusiast circles, the latter is infinitely the better known by its name and might be the outright winner in any competition for the 'name of names'. Occasionally a long-abandoned name has even been re-launched with an altered spelling, such as the Dennis Trident/ East Lancs Lolyne. Other re-spelt names have included East Lancs's Spryte

(though offering no competition to 1960s Austin-Healey sports cars) and its relative, the even more puzzling Flyte.

Of yesterday's and today's buses, the National and Dart names will doubtless also go into the Hall of Fame. But there are plenty of very successful designs that have sold very well but which have remained relatively anonymous — the RE and VR, for example. Giving something a good name doesn't necessarily make it sell well, and, conversely, a bus can become a design classic whilst still having an odd identity.

So it's all a bit of a mess. As radio broadcaster the late John Ebden used to say, after considering the matter we can come to no particular conclusion. We will probably always have chaos, with an indiscriminate muddle of manufacturers' names, nicknames, chassis codes, LT-style class names and seemingly random terms drawn from mythology, the varied worlds of ocean liners, birds, missiles and wild animals, and whatever else comes along. In any case, we now live in a world of rather strange transport names — Thameslink, c2c, Tramlink, 767s, people-carriers, Beetles, tubes, Parcelforce, to cite but a few. Would anyone care to guess the names of the most successful bus designs in the year 2020?

With a predilection for strange spellings featuring the letter 'y', East Lancs called this body the Spryte. It is on a Dennis Dart for Express Travel of Liverpool. *Stewart J. Brown*

ROSSENDALE
MISCELLANY

Rossendale Transport is one of the more out-of-the-way fleets among the few surviving local-authority-owned bus businesses in Britain, although its services do stretch out quite a way from its Rawtenstall base. *W. M. Ewing* illustrates a selection of the vehicles which were in operation in the 1990s

Above: Most of the small number of minibuses in the Rossendale fleet at the end of the decade were Optare MetroRiders, with three batches delivered in 1993, 1994 and 1997. A 1993 bus shows the Handyrider name used on small buses.

Left: Low-floor buses are branded 'Easyride', and the first of these were five Dennis Dart SLFs with East Lancs Spryte bodies in 1996. The location is Bury Interchange.

Above: **At one time Leyland Atlanteans, including some second hand examples, figured prominently. This Alexander-bodied bus, photographed in Rawtens... was new to South Yorkshire PT...**

Left: **All Atlanteans bought new Rossendale were bodied by East Lancs. This is one of a trio purchased in 1980.**

Below: **Although generally similar the East Lancs-bodied Atlantean bought new, this vehicle came Eastbourne. The opening front upper-deck windows were perhaps more suited to the milder and climes of the South Coast than weather which obtains in the Rossendale valley.**

Above: There were also Atlanteans which originated with neighbouring Greater Manchester Transport. This example came from Stagecoach Manchester and is seen in 1998. It has Northern Counties bodywork.

Below: Among the more unusual buses in the fleet were two long-wheelbase Leyland Olympians with coach-style East Lancs bodies. These were bought by Eastbourne Transport in 1985 for operation on an express service to London. They joined the Rossendale fleet in 1993, re-seated with 82 bus seats.

AT THE SHARP END

Back in 1961, a young *David Wayman* joined London Transport as a bus conductor. He looks back at the experience in the days of Routemasters, Gibson ticket machines and pounds, shillings and pence.

They welcome him with open arms. He may be a callow, freckle-faced young guy from deep within the cave-dwelling provinces, but when he announces that he wants to be a bus conductor they practically hug and kiss him. They are chronically and seriously short of platform staff at London Transport in the new year of 1961.

They take down his particulars and begin the processing bit. This takes some days. They give him an aptitude test. They put him through a medical examination and measure him for a uniform. He applies to the Commissioner of Police for the Metropolis to get a conductor's licence, naming two referees. And then after all this there are several days of training at *Chiswick*. Oh, talk about Paradise Found! That's it, the centre of London Transport Executive's bus universe, birthplace of wonderful ideas and location of the celebrated skid-pan, where trainee drivers try unsuccessfully to overturn RT98.

If we'd looked in on London just two months previously, on 8 November 1960, we should have seen the last of the stately trolleybuses at Hanwell gliding silently into the shed after their final journeys on routes 607 and 655. Next day, under Stage 8 of the £10 million trolleybus-replacement scheme,

gleaming new Routemasters would succeed them on renumbered routes 207 and 255 respectively, along with a new variant of the former, designated 207A. Our befreckled bus fan from the back of beyond will be allocated to Hanwell garage, coded HL, although Turnham Green (V) and Shepherds Bush (S) are nearer to his new home. Chiswick, coded CS but not an operational garage, is within walking distance.

Eagerly does he digest fare tables, fill in waybills, calculate sums of money and take on board the intricacies of the 11-day working fortnight, along with the rules, policies and practices relating to the capital's methods of bus operation. His post-Chiswick work will be performed only on Routemasters, but the simulated service journey during training days is made aboard a lovely prewar RT in the driving-school fleet. A learner driver is at the wheel, and all the trainee conductors will play the part of passengers. Each in turn gets to grips with the Gibson ticket machine while trying not to fall about the moving bus.

The RT heads west on Chiswick High Road and soon meets route 65 coming along Kew Bridge Road from Ealing. They follow the 65's course over the Thames at Kew Bridge, through Richmond and toward Kingston. ("Ham Common?" "Yes, we all eat it.") The 65 then proceeds to Surbiton, Chessington and Leatherhead, but the old RT peels off to Norbiton garage (NB). The training inspector calls it *Nawbitn*. A good-old cuppa is enjoyed by all in the canteen.

Now, our cave lad is already familiar with London's transport, thanks to earlier visits to the capital and a sojourn in it. He's been fascinated by London's superb, comprehensive travel network with its frequent services and numerous facilities for interchange within and between modes. He's been spellbound by the highly-standardised LT fleet of

Left: **Trolleybus days, with an all-Leyland vehicle from 1937 which was based at Hanwell depot. The 607 trolleybus route became the 207 when motorbuses took over.** *John Fozard*

buses, some 7,000-strong and covering an operating area of more than 600 square miles. His travels have included regular samples of RTs, RTLs, lowbridge RLHs and trolleybuses.

This, however, is wild boy's first experience of a prewar RT, and he observes its front and rear 'roof boxes'. He notes also the presence of ceiling bell-pushes in the lower saloon. The postwar RT family and RMs have full-length cord bell-pulls, which he considers terribly antiquated. A couple of shifts on Routemasters will change his opinion. He'll then believe that the cord cannot be bettered for quick signal operation by a busy conductor trying to do several things at once. In contrast, the upper saloons of the RT family and RM have only one bell-push, situated at the top of the stairs. This is intended to ensure that, when giving starting signals from the upper saloon, the conductor is in the best position to obtain a clear view of the platform in the staircase mirror. Although involving extra mileage on foot for the conductor — for example when having to interrupt fare-collecting at the front in order to give the signal — it is in the interests of

passenger safety. Giving starting signals by stamping on the floor above the cab, or kicking the interior panelling at the front, are strictly outlawed.

After Chiswick, our primitive specimen and his colleagues go to their respective garages for on-road training and route-learning under the supervision of experienced conductors. Hanwell, in trolleybus and tram tradition, still calls itself a *depot*, although that term will be used interchangeably with *garage* in this account. Old Joe Grant is given responsibility for provincial boy's initiation into the highways and byways of the 207 and 255, then

Right: **A 207 heads for Uxbridge at the end of the 1960s in a scene with remarkably little traffic.** *David Wayman collection*

Below: **Another late-1960s view of the author's old stamping-ground – in this case Shepherds Bush Green.** *R. F. Mack*

Open platforms allowed for speedy loading, as a Routemaster demonstrates in 1980. Note the advert 'Buses need drivers' – a reminder that driver recruitment has long been a challenge for London's bus operators. *David Wayman*

jovial Fred Baker is his mentor for a day on the 207A.

Other than for one digit and all the vehicles, bus routes 207 and 255 are unchanged from trolleybus 607 and 655 respectively. London Transport does try where possible to give replacement bus services new route numbers that bear at least some resemblance to the old ones in the 500s and 600s used for trolleybus routes. The new 207, with its high volume of passenger traffic, has a peak requirement of 53 buses for its length of 12½ miles. A further 20 run on new route 207A at the busiest times.

While almost all eastbound 207 journeys go to Shepherds Bush Green, a fair proportion of westbound ones don't travel the full route to Uxbridge but turn short at Hayes End and in some cases Southall (Delamere Road). On the Hayes End-Shepherds Bush section, at busiest times the frequency may be as high as two minutes. Between Hayes (The Grapes) and the Bush, route 207A is co-ordinated with 207, as is the 255 between Hanwell Broadway and Acton Vale. It is said that with a length of 14.8 miles, the peculiarly-shaped 655 had been London's longest trolleybus route, although single journeys may seldom (if ever) have operated over its entire length. And now, with all this priceless information in his head, it's 'in at the deep end' for primæval forest man. He's a fully-fledged London bus conductor, wearing green-edged badge No N80280, and is let loose on the

unsuspecting bus-riding population. Like Prime Minister Macmillan, he thinks they've never had it so good.

So much for the introduction. Now we look back in normal narrative fashion from our more enlightened age, using the appropriate tenses. 'Tense' describes prehistoric youth's mood on that dark January morning, when his chief concern was what fares to charge without having to spend time consulting the fare table on that initiating journey aboard RM532 in the hands of local veteran driver Jack Gooderham. Fortunately, London Transport, in the Central Area at least, had been able to space its fare stages about half a mile apart and therefore charge the same amount for any given number of stages. As these were numbered consecutively, with no missing numbers, it was as easy to learn as a multiplication table. The structure was: two stages for 3d, three for 5d, four for 6d, six for 8d, eight for 10d, ten for 1s.

During the first few journeys on each route, a keen look-out at stops for the names of nearby thoroughfares, pubs and suchlike made it easy to remember which bus stops lay between which fare stages. At Chiswick, trainees had been told not to ask passengers "how much they paid last time" but to consult the fare table. Having it in one's head saved a bit of time. There was another point to remember too: the system had two types of bus stop, compulsory and request. Signs that were white and red respectively indicated which was which. The bus *had* to come to a stand at a white stop, full or empty, late or early and whether or not passengers intended to board or alight.

The giving of two rings before a clear stop in order to keep the bus moving and save a few seconds was strictly a 'bookable' offence, although that did not, of course, ensure it was never done. At a request stop, intending passengers were required to give a clear hand signal for the bus to stop. Those wishing to get off the bus had to ring the bell once themselves, unless the conductor had already done it. Signalling either from within or without was not necessary in the case of a compulsory stop. The bus was supposed to move off from either kind of stop only upon a two-ring bell signal from the conductor.

On that initial journey from Hanwell to the Bush only a few early-morning travellers hopped on our bus. They boarded our Routemaster mostly in ones and twos, alighting in larger numbers either near their work premises or at interchange points. Many were women with cleaning jobs, and good fun they always were too.

Shepherds Bush Green was a calling point or destination for bus routes 12, 49, 71, 72, 72A, 88, 220 and 268 and trolleybus route 657. Nearby Wells Road was the location of Shepherds Bush LT garage, as well as the terminus of bus routes 105 and the celebrated 11. Routemasters from Shepherds Bush worked the 220 and 268, formerly trolleybus routes 630 and 626/628 respectively. These had been operated until 19 July 1960 by trolleybuses from Hammersmith depot (HB), which closed next day upon the implementation of replacement programme Stage 7. Trolleybuses from Isleworth (IH) ran on the 657. Except where RM and RF types are indicated, all bus routes mentioned here and below were operated by the RT family. As if all these bus services were not enough, there were also two tube stations at Shepherds Bush.

On that first morning our steed, RM532, left Shepherds Bush Green for Uxbridge just before 6am with a few more early morning workers aboard. We were to pick up small numbers at subsequent stops for several miles. The 207 route remained on the road linking Shepherds Bush with Uxbridge, the A4020. Most of the localities penetrated by the 207 were densely populated and contained pockets of industry along with busy shopping areas and many further bus and rail interchange points, all generating passenger traffic. Our Routemaster-operated weekday route 207A from Chelsea or, evenings, from Shepherds Bush Green, kept to the same road as far as Hayes (The Grapes).

RT-family buses on weekday route 12 and Sunday 49 also accompanied RMs on the 207 but only for the first mile, after which they turned right into Old Oak Road. Here we crossed the boundary from London County Council's area into that of Middlesex County Council (an authority that was to disappear under the 1965 London-area reorganisation), although as far as Hanwell we'd still be in the London postal district. We entered Acton Vale at this point, and part way along Acton Vale we came to the terminus of the other Routemaster route operated from our depot, the weekday 255. This was at the junction with Bromyard Avenue (distance 1.3 miles and scheduled running time nine minutes — somewhat slack! — from Shepherds Bush Green for the 207).

The skid-pan at Chiswick was impressive to see, although no still picture is able to capture the drama of a double-deck bus spinning around with its brakes locked. In 1983 a former Routemaster coach is subjected to the skid-pan punishment. *David Wayman*

LUT adopted a new form of traction in 1901, and the result was electrifying. Three years later it completed the extension to Uxbridge. The tram route, which terminated here, became the haunt of the fast and famous 'Feltham'-type double-deck bogie cars, from 1931 until trolleybuses ousted them in 1936.

Our Routemaster ambled ahead. It stopped at Ealing Common station (3.5 miles and 17min from start) for one or two more folk, although a teatime call here would often result in a fill-up from packed trains arriving at three- to four-minute intervals. It was then only a short hop to Ealing Broadway (4 miles), after which we continued past the premises of coach operator Valiant of Ealing.

Now we were in West Ealing and, soon, Hanwell. Gradually, yawning passengers were climbing aboard RM532 in greater numbers. Their conductor stifled his own yawns. Then came Hanwell Broadway (5.5 miles, 28min), location of our depot.

Down the hill we went and crossed the bridge spanning the Brent, one of several Thames

The 255 was a complex affair running in different sections at different times. Its RMs turned here, stayed with the 207s westbound to Hanwell and then steered left for Brentford.

Acton Vale, with a fair amount of industry, then became Acton High Street, a busy shopping centre with Acton Central BR station a few minutes' walk away. We climbed gently past the Town Hall (2.5 miles from the start).

Reminding us of times before the advent of trolleybuses, our RM passed the former Acton tram shed, during this period a works depot. Horse trams had operated between Shepherds Bush and Acton High Street from 1876, reaching the newly-opened shed in 1895, when the organisation had been in the hands of London United Tramways for a year.

tributaries. We had now reached the dual carriageway, on the opposite side of which a Routemaster was to misbehave some time later. It was the morning rush hour, and, with full standing load, McManus — never a laggard — had his foot down trying to keep ahead of a line of cars racing toward the reverse curves before the bridge. Ah yes, but our bus that day would be RM553, queerest of the breed at Hanwell in those days. At this kind of speed it would and now did develop a severe front-end judder. The steering column joined in the convulsing with the handbrake, which, mounted on the left of the cab and close to the sliding window, was testing the strength of the glass with violent hammer-blows. McManus could restore normality only by bringing the speed down. There was to be no further opportunity for such entertainment all the way to the Bush.

Back on RM532 heading west, Southall garage (HW) stood on the right, terminus of the 92 group of routes serving Greenford and parts of Wembley. The Iron Bridge lay ahead, carrying the Western Region main line over the A4020 road and proclaiming the fact that AEC's premises were on the left. At Lyndhurst Avenue, a short distance beyond, AEC workers would alight, usually from slightly later journeys.

Forward we bore to Southall Town Hall (7 miles). This was at a busy junction with South Road to the left and Lady Margaret Road to the right. It was also an interchange point with three routes: crossing our path were the 105, which we'd seen briefly at the

Bush and at peak times would see again shortly, and the 232; the 120 terminated here during normal hours. Half a mile or so further on, between the bridges over the Grand Union Canal (Paddington branch) and the Yeading Brook, we reached the junction with Delamere Road, where a few 207 journeys terminated (7.5 miles, 39min from the Bush).

Soon we reached The Grapes (9 miles), a large hostelry at a slightly staggered junction (not the only thing that staggered late at night). We were now in the Middlesex Hayes, not to be confused with its namesake on the other side of LT Central Area in Kent. Yeading Lane went to the right and Coldharbour Lane to the left. Our own 207A turned left here and would reach Hayes station within five minutes. It was straight ahead for us on the 207, however, and RM532 continued west-north-westerly along the northern outskirts of Hayes.

The population density was thinning a little now, reflected by the terminating of many 207 journeys at Hayes End, just ahead (practically 10 miles from the Bush, 47min scheduled running time). There was always less bustle hereabouts, and drivers of Uxbridge-bound RMs would seize the opportunity to

The idea that buses could be 30ft long was received with some incredulity by the author's workmates. But they could, and the standard RM was lengthened to make the 30ft-long RML by adding a short bay in the centre of the body, which increased seating capacity to 72. This is a 1966 RML at Ludgate Circus in 1988. The last of the standard short RMs entered service in 1965. *David Wayman*

While Routemasters may have disappeared from the Uxbridge Road, the type has led a charmed existence, surviving into the 21st century. A London Central example heads out of Trafalgar Square on its way to Peckham, carrying branding for route 12. *David Wayman*

make up any time lost on the busier and more congested sections further east.

Shortly we came to Hillingdon (10.5 miles), where we reached the steepest descent of the whole route, Hillingdon Hill, with Hillingdon Church at the top and the bridge spanning the River Pinn at the foot. Some 300 yards long, at about 1 in 14, the drop was nothing compared with some of the Pennine plunges on bus routes around Halifax and Huddersfield, for example. A little further on, to our right, lay Uxbridge LT station at the end of two LT Underground branch lines, the Piccadilly and the Met. RM532 then had only a step to take along the A4020, leading to Denham, accompanied by some green Country Area routes. By the Fray's River Bridge (12.5 miles, 61min), practically at the Middlesex/ Buckinghamshire boundary and a few hundred yards short of LT's Uxbridge garage, it reached the 207 terminus, where we could enjoy a short rest.

Oh, but what a bus, the Routemaster! Integrally constructed with Park Royal aluminium alloy-framed bodywork, the standard RM specification called for AEC running units incorporating the AV590 9.6-litre engine, along with fully automatic transmission; some later examples had the Leyland O.600 9.8-litre engine. Coil-spring suspension which was

independent at the front, power-assisted steering, ergonomic cab and heating in both saloons were also specified. Those early RMs were 27ft 6in long and 8ft wide, with a wheelbase of 16ft 10in and seating for 64 (36 above, 28 below), six fewer than on the standard trolleybus. Their unladen weight was officially 7¼ tons, of which the nominal weight of a seated load, exactly 4 tons, was 55%. This compared well with the heavier, 56-seat RTW type of bus, for example, where the figure was only 43%.

It could be argued that, of 1950s-designed double-deckers conceived and built to be of moderately light weight, the Routemaster was possibly the most well-finished and well-appointed. The seating, moquette-covered with leathercloth trim, was up to London Transport's usual standard of comfort. Gangways were of a width convenient for the movement of passengers and conductor. That in the lower saloon was 20in wide at cushion level and 28in at seat-top level, the difference being due to the taper of the seat frame's outer edge. The upper saloon measurements were 1½in less because of the slightly diminishing width of the upper saloon toward the roof.

The first production Routemaster (RM8) had appeared at the 1958 Commercial Motor Show, and one enterprising municipal-transport general manager wrote later that he considered it the best bus at the exhibition. To some extent it seemed a contradiction that another star of that show was the new rear-engined Leyland Atlantean, of which four examples were displayed in the form to which the model had then evolved. Understandably, Leyland

Motors' publicity sought to persuade operators that the future of double-deck bus operation lay in this model, embodying what was then seen as a revolutionary back-to-front entrance/engine layout. However, London saw the RM as its own 'bus of the future'. The possible contradiction lay in the fact that, for all the advanced nature of its specification, the standard RM stuck to the tried and tested format, even to the extent of retaining an open platform. Although by no means all operators were won over to rear-engined models immediately, and some even reverted to front-engined types after sampling the new concept, the eventual outcome is a matter of history. Now, in the 21st century, it is clear that the mid-20th-century Routemaster has proved incredibly long-lasting and admirably suited to the peculiar needs of the capital.

Routemasters had made their first full-scale appearance at the fourth stage of the trolleybus replacement plan, on 11 November 1959, involving West Ham and Poplar depots. After the trolleys had gone RMs began replacing RT types, and there was a dispute between the crews' union and LT. The crews wanted one-for-one replacement, whereas LT wanted to replace every 11 members of the RT family with 10 RMs. Eventually LT conceded.

During the postwar era, although the standard of organisation was excellent, London's road-transport network was bedevilled by two factors. One was increasing road traffic congestion, leading to frequent service delays and gaps left by buses that were being turned short of their destination in order to recover lost time. The other was platform-staff shortage, which had become endemic and was a recurrent cause of cancelled journeys, also creating service gaps which then led to delays on account of the heavier burdens being left for following buses.

During one afternoon rush hour I was on route 207A with Sean, the two factors combining to retard our progress. Bound for Chelsea (Stanley Arms), we left Hayes station (actual stop Clarendon Road) on time for what should have been a normal (if busy) 70min trip. Five minutes into the journey, when we joined the Uxbridge Road at The Grapes, we found that we 'had a road on', the crews' term for picking up unusually heavy loadings. This was because a 207 from Uxbridge to Shepherds Bush was missing in front of us and then, east of Hanwell Broadway, so was a 255 from Brentford to Acton Vale. The 207 that was scheduled ahead of the 255 was also following a gap and, of course, leaving folk standing, increasing our own turnover of passengers even further. Abnormally heavy road traffic added to the problem. As usual in such circumstances, lateness became cumulative, leading to bunching. On the day in question, we were about 15min late at the Bush, and an

The 607 route number was revived in more recent times for a limited-stop service from Uxbridge to Shepherds Bush. A Leyland National 2 on the 607 Express heads out of Uxbridge in 1995. *Stewart J. Brown*

inspector there authorised us to turn back at South Kensington station, which, in theory, should have regained us about 17min. (The few passengers we had aboard for stops beyond that point were transferred to an RT on route 49.) On our return journey, we were still late leaving South Ken. With further exceptional congestion and other buses missing ahead, we lost more time and ended up being turned at Southall. This gained us more than 20 minutes, but, even so, we were only just back on schedule when relieved at Hanwell.

Watching some of Hanwell's long-serving drivers would often raise a smile. Bleary-eyed, they'd greet one another at dawn with an affectionate "Mawnin', you old ****!". (It sounded like 'bar steward'.) The oldest of them was then 70. Many had driven trolleybuses for countless ages, and some had been tram drivers before that. One of them believed that, although the Routemasters were "*awl right, they wouldn't lahst as long as the ol' trolleys*".

But talk about teaching old dogs new tricks! One motor-bus characteristic that they seemed stubbornly reluctant to accept was that it could overtake the one in front. Officialdom frowned on the practice between vehicles on the same route, as it put them out of sequence. The handbook instruction was that, if a bus was running late and the following one caught up, the latter should drop back in order to restore headway. This, of course, may have been sound advice during earlier decades, but in the traffic conditions of the early 1960s it was useless. A late runner could usually be helped to regain some time if the following bus overtook and picked up some of the load, which, of course, would usually have grown during the longer wait. These old-timers, however, would stay behind with their snouts almost up the staircase of the preceding bus, three minutes or three days behind time. But if there was one thing that all drivers appreciated, it was a mate who was quick on the starting bells.

Liam was the driver with whom I was eventually paired, soon after he graduated from Chiswick

Below: **London Transport is but a memory, and its successor in West London is FirstGroup. Before the adoption of 'First' as a fleetname, a 1967 RML from CentreWest heads through Central London with 'Gold Arrow' fleetnames and FirstGroup's 'f' logo.** *Stewart J. Brown*

Right: **The 207 remains a trunk route today. If the author's colleagues baulked at the prospect of 30ft Routemasters, what would they have made of articulated buses measured in metres (all 18 of them) ? The 207 was selected for a trial of articulated buses in the winter of 2001/2. FirstGroup provided six Volvos with Wright bodies, borrowed from its Glasgow and Southampton fleets. This one is at Hayes.** *Stewart J. Brown*

Driving School. After reading in *Buses Illustrated* about the plan to introduce Routemasters of 30ft length, I mentioned this to Liam. He was incredulous. How did LT expect drivers to manage in heavy traffic? He'd forgotten that trolleybus drivers were still managing it with their charges. I just left it at that. Didn't want anyone mistaking me for a transport enthusiast, did I?

Before pairing with Liam I'd been Ernie Varley's conductor for a few weeks while his permanent 'clippie', Elsie, was off sick. A personable West Londoner, Ernie was a good, steady driver who didn't throw his mate about the bus — unlike Liam, who could cause the odd bruise or two. One morning, Ernie and I had RM563 on a 255 over at Clapham Junction. Our wires became crossed, and, unusually, he set off from the terminus without a bell signal. Indeed, he couldn't have received one, as his mate was in the public convenience! Ernie realised this at the first stop and waited until a breathless conductor caught up.

Regrettably, Liam's methods occasionally seemed to indicate some amnesia since his driving school days, and, well, his style perhaps may have lacked some finesse. This was illustrated in Acton High Street one afternoon. When passing a stationary car — granted, it was a wide, gaudy American thing — he did a minor re-shaping job on its panelling. RM545 was scarred a little too. Several days later, at Ealing Common, a passenger introduced himself to me as a plain-clothes driving instructor, sent to observe Liam. He'd been aboard from the Bush and clearly wasn't too happy, even pointing out a few of the reasons why. The upshot of this was that Liam was returned to Chiswick for a refresher course, following which matters improved somewhat.

Collecting fares could be speeded up by one-handed operation of the excellent Gibson ticket machine. The fare-selector knob and release trigger were on the left, the operating handle on the right. When the trigger was pressed, the handle and the knob became locked on the central spindle and both revolved together. It was a simple matter to select the fare and then, with a deft left-thumb and whole-hand action, flick the knob around and churn out a blizzard of tickets while the right hand remained free to deal with cash. I reckoned it could save a couple of seconds or so on each transaction, and, with the inrush of a sudden heavy load, that could be valuable. This was especially so on eastbound 207 journeys at the King's Arms in Acton Vale when the AEI factory workers and others were coming out, for they'd usually fill both saloons and most would have their tanners ready for a 5d fare to the Bush. Using the right fingers to take and pocket the tendered coin while holding a supply of pennies in the palm, the two-handed drill would be: "5d?"; (1) flick machine knob/take and pocket coin; (2) hand ticket/give 1d change; "Thankyou!" — quicker than it takes to read that. Passengers would often stare, and some asked whether the machines were now battery-operated! My record number of ticket issues was on 30 March 1961 (Maundy Thursday), with more than 1,300 clocked on a 207 shift. As about 200 of these would have been 'combination' tickets (two joined, of 1s 2d value or higher), that would have meant perhaps some 1,200 passengers, averaging 20 or so per mile.

Well, that was all a year or two ago now, and I have since returned to the provinces.

And Routemasters? They've just kept going on.

CHANGING FORTUNES FOR EUROPEAN TROLLEYBUSES

Trolleybuses in Europe face a varied future, secure in some places, uncertain in others. *Tony Moyes* takes a look.

All photographs by the author

Maybe because trolleybuses disappeared from public service in Britain almost 30 years ago, British trolleybus enthusiasts seem to have been more internationally minded than motorbus enthusiasts. Alan Murray's *World Trolleybus Encyclopædia*, published in 2000, provides a tantalising record of the global state of the beast and will surely encourage more of us to visit some rather unlikely tourist destinations —

the Russian equivalents of Bedwas & Machen, for example.

Much has been made of the trolleybus's 'green' credentials; a Lausanne timetable describes the trolleybus as '*l'ami public numéro un*'. Yet European systems face persistent problems of coping with unsympathetic highway planners, deregulation, ownership changes and (particularly in Eastern Europe) rising electricity prices and replacement

costs. So, as in Britain, in many European cities that opted for trolleybuses, once the first generation of equipment wore out, out it went and is now a memory; typically for France, for example, two of the modest little Vetra VBRhs that inaugurated the small three-route system at Brest in 1947 ran until it closed in 1970, daily using complex insulated overhead on the Pont de Récouvrance lifting bridge in the process.

Trolleybuses were once so widespread in mainland Europe that it was common to come across systems by accident, and casual photographs of them would be grabbed on the spur of the moment. Information seemed hard to come by — and yet from 1971 there was Robert Jowitt's book *Silence of Trolleybuses* to inspire. Since then a fair number of systems have vanished but some new ones have appeared, as at Ghent, or reappeared, as at Innsbruck. Now that there is a plethora of information available via *Trolleybus Magazine* and the Trolleynet website, why not taste a selection of what was — and in some cases still is — available?

In broadly alphabetical order, let us start with the city of Arnhem, last survivor of only three systems in the Netherlands. It illustrates well the changing marques of chassis, body and electrics available: these are increasingly short-run adaptations of bus chassis. The network opened on 5 September 1949, starting with two-axle BUT 9721Ts, some of which lasted up to 20 years. Verheul-bodied No 101 survives in preservation. The last British chassis were eight two-axle Leyland LVB6Ts new in 1968. As is often the case in mainland Europe, the station forecourt is a good focal point in the network. By 1985 Arnhem had received 31 'pure' Den Oudstens with Kiepe electrics — adapted B79 buses, in effect — the oldest of which have ended up in Rostov-on-Don. It is testimony to the growing complexity of electrical and electronic control gear that there seem to be many more teething troubles with new models than with simpler, older types. Ten Berkhofs were originally due in January 2001, but, to provide a realistic production volume, a joint order was placed with the undertaking in Solingen, Germany, of which more anon. Arnhem's distinctive dark-blue livery has so far survived merger of the town and regional public transport systems, although by early 2002 the peak vehicle requirement was down to 27.

Norway too has just one surviving trolleybus system, in Bergen. Since it started in 1950, more than 70 new vehicles have passed through the system, with a maximum of 29 in use at any one time. Unusually, Bergen had 20 Skoda 9Trs, representing one of the few exports of this Czech-built workhorse outside the former Comecon countries. Four Volvo B58s arrived in the 1970s; then there were three MANs and three Mercedes-Benz, followed in mid-1985 by three MAN/Gräf & Stifts (G&S being the Austrian arm of MAN — see later under Salzburg). The system's mileage has greatly declined, despite strong environmentalist support. By September 2001, the fleet was down to six pure trolleybuses and two dual-mode duobuses.

With 14 surviving systems, Switzerland has Western Europe's greatest concentration of trolleybuses. Characteristically, that at Bern began with some tram routes, being converted in 1941. Trams and cross-city trolleybus route 12 both use the attractive Marktgaße and Spitalgaße through the old city. There are three radial routes from the Hauptbahnhof, two of which may revert to tram by 2004, and a working fleet of about 40. This has included models from FBW (standing for Franz Bronzincevic of Wetzikon), manufacturer of many

Swiss trolleybuses until merged with Saurer and Mercedes in 1982 under the title of NAW in a bid to survive in a rather intermittent market place.

Doyenne of the Swiss systems continues to be Lausanne, an attractive conurbation of a quarter of a million people that shelves down to Lake Geneva. Urban trolleybuses were first introduced in 1932 but did not finally replace city trams until 1964. Transports Lausannois (TL) also had three quite long rural electric tramways with thinnish irregular frequencies; two were eventually converted to trolleybus, though they did not exactly shout their presence. In 1984 the overhead stretched far into the distance beyond the Epalignes trolley terminus, apparently carrying just four route 21 trolleys per day onwards to Chalet à Gobet, but there was no hint in the timetables that these were trolleybus-worked. But peak-hour jam-packed trolleys would still be making fairly slow progress uphill northwards on route 20 bound for Montheron, 15 minutes beyond the busy suburban Bellevaux trolleybus terminal, and the neat timetable booklet left no doubt that this was a trolleybus service. Accounts vary of how long the 20 (now 60) stayed electrified; road works in the early 1990s played havoc, and there was a legal spat over a turning circle. Authority to remove the overhead was granted in the late 1990s after what was described as five years of disuse. The otherwise excellent TL website is not clear on the current (no pun intended) position. Urban route extensions have subsequently taken place and are in prospect, however, though it is said that the fleet could be cut to 80 once a batch of Neoplan duobuses is delivered. A new rapid-transit line has also siphoned off some of the trade

of the existing routes. In perhaps three respects, TL resembles the erstwhile Bradford Corporation. Firstly, its trolleybuses were traditionally light blue. Secondly, it had an eye to a bargain. When systems like Zurich and Geneva switched to articulated trolleybuses, Lausanne bought displaced small two-axle vehicles; some of these were 50 years old when withdrawn. In 1974 TL even reused components from prewar trolleys in 18 otherwise brand-new FBW/Hess/SAAS models. Thirdly, its routes are hilly, and to cope with things there's a viaduct across the city centre of which Bradford might have been envious. In another respect, Lausanne is unusual for Switzerland in having only one (experimental) articulated trolleybus in the fleet at present. It has stayed loyal to trailers, 50 new ones having been bought in 1987. At the end of 2001 the average age of the 106-vehicle trolleybus fleet was 19.2 years.

In contrast to Lausanne, the small, neat trolleybus network in Lugano at the southern end of Switzerland closed on 28 June 2001, dogged by costs of replacing vehicles and electrical equipment — it used an unusual 1000V DC electrical system. Trolleys had started on 25 April 1954 and had replaced and reached beyond the last urban trams in December 1959. Penny numbers of vehicles were delivered up to 1988 — mixed artics and two-axled, generally FBWs at first, followed by Volvos and finally Vetters. The most modern ones, along with substations and overhead, have been sold to Brasov in Romania.

Moving to Austria, Salzburg has had more than 60 years of trolleybus operation, and it remains large-scale. It has been particularly populated by

Left: **A 1949 FFA-bodied FBW with MFO electrics in Lausanne. This bus was new to Zurich and after 10 years passed to Geneva, reaching Lausanne in 1975. It is seen at Place St François.**

Above: **A 1957 FBW/SWS/BBC new to Zurich is seen in Lausanne in 1982, being followed by an FBW/Hess/Secheron, one of 20 delivered that year.**

Above: Trolleybuses with trailers are a feature of Lausanne, as shown by an FBW with an old-style trailer.

Below: A rather more modern trailer is being pulled by one of Lausanne's 1982 FBW/Hess/Secherons fitted with a rather noisy Volkswagen auxiliary petrol engine.

Gräf & Stifts: MAN has used this Austrian subsidiary to produce trolleybuses. Steyr (at the time Daimler-Benz's equivalent Austrian arm) got a look-in at the more recent purchases.

At its maximum, Germany had 88 trolleybus systems, of which only seven remain. In 1993 Solingen, on the southern edge of the Ruhr, had 67 MAN trolleybuses (assembled in Austria), of which 21 were artics, dating from 1984-7 and replacing a fleet that had itself replaced trams between 1952 and 1959. As mentioned under Arnhem, some Berkhofs are on order, constituting a third generation. There is a web of branches and loops centring on Solingen itself, but the handiest route is probably the 9.5km-long trunk 683 which runs from a terminus in the next town of Wuppertal-Vohwinkel, right beneath the famous suspended railway, or Schwebebahn, up hill and down dale to central Solingen, where the big rigid MAN six-wheeler was caught, and thence southeast to Burg, where there is a turntable.

Some 15km to the north of Solingen, in the midst of Germany's Ruhr district, the city of Essen until recently boasted a fascinating essay in trolleybus technology. Since 1967, trams on 600V DC have burrowed under the city centre in a subway. Experiments with guided articulated diesel buses had begun in 1983, following which the subway was equipped with guideways and 750V DC trolleybus overhead. Eighteen Daimler-Benz O405GTD articulated duobuses entered service in November 1986. Because of underground derailments and vehicle unreliability, the subway reverted to tram-only in September 1995, and the duobuses thereafter normally ran in guided and unguided diesel mode on the surface only. The overhead equipment was kept for demonstration purposes, but the duobuses ended their days as buses on intermittent on-street tram-replacement work; they were withdrawn in September 2001, and most were promptly sold to a Russian dealer. Within the subway, the overhead was carried on the flanks of the tunnel roof. On the surface, this route was covered largely in unguided diesel mode. Riding the subway at speed in one of these vehicles was a most curious experience; outside, it was as gloomy as the London Underground. The main sound was the low rhythmic thump of the tyres on the joints in the guideway, and if you looked out of the back window, a tram might well be on your tail not far behind. A duobus system, originally with 20 duobuses and four pure trolleybuses, remains in operation at Esslingen, much further south in Germany, though one hears

Left: **A Lugano FBW seen heading for Castagnola in 1988.**

Above: **Also in Lugano in 1988, a more modern Hess-bodied Volvo.**

Below: **As the source of a fair proportion of Lausanne's stock, Zurich deserves a glimpse. This is a Zurich artic near Central Station in August 1984. It is one of 30 FBWs bodied by Ramseier & Jenzer and delivered in 1974 with distinctive lantern windscreens. Trolleybuses first appeared in the city in May 1939 but still play second fiddle to trams.**

Above and right: Rigid and articulated Gräf & Stift trolleybuses in the Salzburg fleet.

Below: A newly-delivered articulated Vetter/Vetter/Secheron SHO18 in the Lugano fleet loads for Breganzona at Pregassona in 1988.

that reliability of the duobuses has been a problem. The message might be to get there quickly before things disappear.

What of the future? There are newish systems. In Belgium, for example, one bus route in Ghent was converted in 1989, and lavish provision made specially for the 18 new Van Hool trolleybuses. In the brand-new depot, for instance, each vehicle had its own numbered bay, like the named places for each steed in racing stables. Ingeniously, the one route manages to overlap the city's dominant tram network only over about 50m of critical junction, and the big vehicles certainly shift the crowds, but the southern end of the route serves an inner-city area liable to renewal at much lower population density. A new regional transport authority seems to tolerate them for the moment, but there was sufficient slack in the system to allow four vehicles to be hired to Arnhem at the end of the 1990s to cover for slow delivery of new stock. The verdict of Arnhem passengers was adverse: spartan, noisy and slow — hardly an accolade for newish vehicles that should have every environmental virtue in their favour. Let us hope that that is a minority view, and that Europe's trolleybuses continue to provide a gene pool of quality urban transport that may yet breed again in the UK.

Above left: **A Solingen trolley in Wuppertal-Vohwinkel, beneath the suspended railway.**

Left: **A big rigid MAN six-wheeler in Solingen.**

Right: **Illustrating the versatility of the Essen duobuses (at least in theory), one emerges from the eastern end of the subway at Volkshochschule in guided-trolleybus mode in September 1993. After running for another 500m as an orthodox on-street trolleybus, it will cover the next 3km as a guided diesel bus, pass through the centre of Kray as an on-street trolleybus and end its journey in unguided diesel mode in eastern Kray.**

Above: **In the subway at Essen, with a duobus running in guided-trolleybus mode at Berliner Platz station.**

Above: **More recent Salzburg deliveries have included vehicles from Steyr. This is one of four 1987 Steyr/Kiepes, bound for Birkensiedlung, which sounds rather like (but isn't anything like) the old Eastern Scottish destination of Birkenside.**

Left: **Ghent depot, with a numbered bay for each bus.**

Right: **One of Ghent's 1989 Van Hool trolleybuses.**

THE 20-PLUS CLUB

A surprising number of elderly vehicles still roam Britain's roads, showing that vehicles which have been looked after well can clock up over 20 years of service. *Geoff Mills* illustrates a selection of golden oldies which were still running in East Anglia in the early years of the 21st century.

Above: **Not quite 20, this youngster was just 18 when photographed in October 2002 in Newmarket. Operated by MD Travelhire of Ipswich, it's a rare Dennis Dorchester with 49-seat Duple Caribbean body. It was new to Gastonia of Cranleigh.**

Left: **Another odd oldie, again not quite 20 years old, is this unusual Quest VM with Riches Coaches of Stradbrooke. The rear-engined Quest was powered by a Ford engine; VM are the initials of Vernon Maitland, owner of Excelsior Coaches of Bournemouth, the coach's original operator. Plaxton Paramount bodywork is fitted, featuring the low driving position which was fashionable for a short time in the early 1980s.**

Above: Getting nearer the 20-year mark is this former United Counties Leyland Leopard PSU5 with Duple Dominant IV body, seen outside Colchester Castle in the ownership of Buckland of Ipswich.

Below: Unique is an over-worked and oft-misused word, but it does apply to this front-engined Volvo B57 with Alexander Y-type body, purchased by Alexander (Northern) of Aberdeen in 1983, when that company was looking for an alternative to the Ford R-series. By 2000 it was running for Alec Head of Lutton, Northamptonshire.

Above: **MAN successfully pioneered the use of continental rear-engined integral coaches in the UK, being the first importer to achieve consistently respectable sales volumes. Its original model was the SR280. Wahl of London took 10 in 1982. This one survived with D-Way Travel of Earsham in the summer of 2000, looking in remarkably nice condition for such a rare survivor.**

Below: **Ford once vied with Bedford for leadership in UK coach sales. In 1981 this R1114 with 53-seat Plaxton Supreme IV body was delivered to Sealandair of West Bromwich. By 2000 it was running for West Row Coaches in Suffolk. The first two digits in the chassis code indicate an 11m-long model.**

Above: East Lancs bodies were never that common on Bristol VRTs. This was one of three bought by Rhymney Valley in 1981, seen 20 years later in the fleet of Colchester Coaches of Clacton-on-Sea. The Rhymney Valley and Bristol businesses have long since gone, but East Lancs is still active and building much more stylish bodies than it did in the 1980s.

Right: Looking as good as new is this 1980 Bedford YLQ in the fleet of Fowlers of Holbeach Drove. The YLQ was a 10m chassis, and the Duple Dominant II body on this coach seated 45. It was new to Kenzies of Shepreth, registered CVE 7V.

Right: In 1980 the Leyland National 2 was the ultimate in single-deck bus design, and Alexander (Fife) took a batch of 12 of the longer (11.6m) version. They were 52-seaters. Caroline-Seagull was operating this former Fife bus in Great Yarmouth in the summer of 2001.

Above: Standard NBC-style ECW-bodied VRTs were fairly rare in most parts of the country at the start of the 21st century. This First example was still operating in Colchester at the end of 2002. It was new in 1978 to South Wales Transport with a Leyland 501 engine, but was later fitted with the more common (and more economical) Gardner 6LXB.

Left: London Transport was a major buyer of the Leyland National, and this one was delivered to the capital in 1977. By 2002 it was running for Neave of Catfield and is seen in service in Norwich.

Above right: Blackpool Transport's standard bus in the late 1970s was the long-wheelbase Leyland Atlantean with East Lancs body. This bus came from the original 1977 batch and is an 86-seater. By 2000 it was operating for Don's of Dunmow.

Right: 'Wish you were here...?' is the trading name of Fosker of Martlesham, which in 2002 was operating this one-time Barton Transport Leyland Leopard dating from 1973, when Barton was taking advantage of the Government's New Bus Grant to modernise its fleet. The two-piece power-operated door was an indication of what was commonly described as a 'grant coach'. The Leyland badge, of a style adopted in 1981, is a later addition.

Above: **The Ulster registration mark disguises the origins of this unusual vehicle. Also part of the fleet of Wish you were here...?, it has a 1974 long-wheelbase Atlantean AN68/2R chassis and started life as SUG 595M in the West Yorkshire PTE fleet. The 46-seat East Lancs body was fitted in 1992 for Hylton Castle of East Boldon, which ran the bus in its Catch-A-Bus fleet.**

Left: **For two decades Nottingham City Transport bought vehicles which were immediately identifiable by a variety of features, including, on this 1974 East Lancs-bodied Atlantean, a solid steel bumper and a forward-angled destination display above a BET-style double-curvature windscreen. It is seen in 2002 in the fleet of Fourways Coaches of Chelmsford.**

Above: In 1971 Aberdeen Corporation bought 20 33ft-long Daimler Fleetlines with Alexander bodywork, originally of dual-door layout. Fords of Althorne operated three buses of this type from 1984 to 2002.

Below: New petrol-engined coaches were becoming rare when this Bedford SBG (G for gasoline) entered service with Chiltonian of Hungerford in 1956. Still running on petrol, this pretty Duple-bodied coach is now owned by Lodges of High Easter and is the oldest PSV in regular use in East Anglia. The location is Colchester Castle.

THE ALLURE OF THE OPEN-TOPPER

There was a time when open-top buses ran only in seaside resorts on the South Coast in the summer. But not any more. *Buses* editor Alan Millar looks at the spread of open-toppers to some unlikely places.

London Transport, bless it, didn't get a lot right in the 1970s. Certainly not when it came to buses. But one of its least remembered yet rare inspired decisions halfway through that dismal decade quite possibly saved and transformed the role of a great British institution that might otherwise have disappeared by now.

I speak of the open-top double-decker. Before 1975, this was almost exclusively a seaside feature. And one largely of the southern English seaside, where the season lasted longer and the weather was more likely to favour a bracing ride along the esplanade aboard a bus that was exposed to the coastal elements. Like so many of those resorts, their numbers there have declined as ever greater numbers of Britons themselves deserted these shores aboard charter holiday jets bound for the warmer delights of the Mediterranean and Adriatic, and later even farther afield. They have largely gone the way of paddle steamers, pleasure piers, variety theatres, kiss-me-quick hats and battleaxe landladies.

In the summer of 1972 London Transport started running open-top tours using five Guy Arab IIIs hired from East Kent. These dated from 1951 and had Park Royal bodies which had been converted to open-top in the 1960s. The fare was 65p.
Stewart J. Brown

Open-toppers were also to be found along the North Wales coast, in Scarborough, Southport and Morecambe, and there were (and still are) open-top trams in Blackpool. Otherwise, one or two others were kept for special occasions like victorious returning football teams touring their home towns with cup held aloft, but there were nowhere near enough of these in the right places at the right time. In 1967, when Glasgow Celtic became the first British team to win the European Cup, the legendary Lisbon Lions drove past the cheering masses on the back of an open coal lorry.

The farther north you encountered them, open-toppers more likely were old buses with their roofs and upper deck windows stripped off, for this was low-mileage work. There was little call for their services outside the height of the summer season. To get around that problem, operators serving the busier southern resorts invested in new convertible open-toppers between 1959 and 1965. These buses' roofs spent the summer stacked awkwardly in corners of garages but could be fitted to keep the buses' wheels turning through the winter on the normal range of public services. As it turned out, Crosville got the first of these, for the North Wales resorts. But the big investment saw Bristol Omnibus (at Weston-super-Mare) and Brighton Hove & District between them take 20 rear-entrance Bristol Lodekkas; Southdown took 30 'Queen Mary' Leyland PD3s, Devon General nine 'Sea Dog' Leyland Atlanteans at Torquay, and Bournemouth 10 Weymann-bodied Daimler Fleetlines.

Even though the traditional British seaside holiday was in steep decline by 1977/8, the National Bus Company commissioned 50 convertible Bristol VRs for Southdown (30), Western National (11), Hants & Dorset (six) and South Wales (three). Bournemouth bought 11 Fleetlines around the same time, but few of those 61 buses were replaced 20 years later.

By 1975 London Transport was breathing new life into the Round London Sightseeing Tour. Staff shortages had led to large-scale sub-contracting to coach operators, but it started using some of its newest Daimler Fleetline double-deckers from 1973, as iconic red double-deckers clearly were a big attraction for foreign visitors. The next step, from April 1975, was to add open-toppers to the tour. The attraction was not so much the thrill of a bracing top-deck ride round London but the opportunity to see and photograph the capital's landmarks from all angles, without bits of the bus getting in the way.

The actual choice of LT's first seven open-toppers was a reflection of the troubled state of the LT fleet, for 1975 was the year it had anticipated withdrawing its last RTs and starting the steady replacement of its by then 16-year-old Routemasters. But the decision to get shot of much newer single-deck Merlins and Swifts had not merely granted another four years' life to the RTs and postponed the

Routemasters' demise indefinitely; it also prompted the purchase of the first of British Airways' surplus forward-entrance Routemasters, and some of these surprise additions were used briefly in revenue-earning service. In other circumstances, maybe a few of the oldest RMLs would have had their tops lopped off for the tour, but they were far too precious for a venture that had still to prove itself, so LT hired in ex-Midland Red D9s dating from between 1960 and 1963.

In some respects the D9 was the next best thing to a Routemaster, another integrally constructed operator-designed, rear-entrance half-cab double-decker that was technically ahead of its time. Aside from looking like a traditional London bus, its greater attraction for the sightseeing tour was that it was one of the few 72-seat rear-entrance models on the second-hand market that also had two-pedal control and platform doors. The latter feature could always have been added to fend off unwanted boarders, but semi- or fully-automatic transmission

Above: **An ex-Bournemouth Fleetline operating on the London Transport sightseeing tour provides a grandstand view of the Changing of the Guard in Whitehall in 1978.** *Stewart J. Brown*

Below: **After service in Bournemouth and London, this Fleetline moved on to join the Guide Friday fleet. It is seen in Stratford in 1991, and was still in use when Ensign took over the Guide Friday business in 2002, by which time it was an amazing 37 years old.** *Alan Millar*

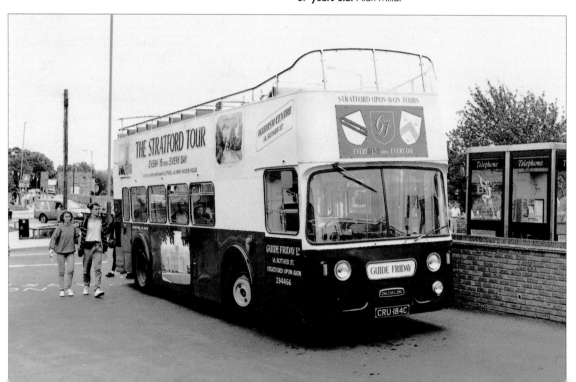

Right: **East Kent had a tradition of running open-top tour buses. This former East Kent AEC Regent V had gravitated to National Travel South East by 1977, when it was repainted silver to mark the monarch's Jubilee.**
Stewart J. Brown

Below: **Open-top buses were long a feature of South Coast resorts, and a number of operators ran convertible open-toppers which could be re-roofed each winter. Among those was Southdown, operator of this 1964 Leyland Titan PD3 with Northern Counties body. The location is Beachy Head in the summer of 1973; while the bus still carries Southdown's green-and-cream livery, its fleetname is in the recently-introduced corporate NBC style.**
Stewart J. Brown

was the norm in London and — above all else — the economic reality of open-top double-deckers is that you can only sell seats upstairs. If the weather is good, nobody wants to sit downstairs. If it turns wet, those sitting upstairs need the option of occupying empty seats downstairs. The D9s had 40 seats on top.

By comparison with what is offered today, those 1975 open-top tours were a bit of an endurance test. You were on the bus for two hours without any courier, commentary or means of escape. Passengers were issued with a printed guide to the main sights in Japanese and six European languages.

Although painted in LT livery, bedecked in exclusive advertising for Johnnie Walker Scotch Whisky and allocated authentic fleetnumbers OM1-7, the D9s were operated by Obsolete Fleet, which bought them from the then relatively small Ensign dealership, then based at Grays. Obsolete Fleet was run by one of the larger-than-life figures of London bus enthusiasm and preservation,

Prince Marshall, a commoner whose parents gave him 'Prince' as a forename. Leon Daniels, one of his right-hand men at Obsolete Fleet, these days heads FirstGroup's London operations.

The D9s were hired initially for three years, and some lingered a bit longer on the short-lived 74Z shuttle between Baker Street station and Regent's Park Zoo. There also was a less successful attempt to keep at least one of them busy on a Christmas Lights tour, but the market wasn't yet ready to be frozen in pursuit of uninterrupted night-time views. The main venture, however, was so successful that LT obtained its own permanent replacements in 1977. To an operator of over 2,600 Daimler/Leyland Fleetlines, it made a certain sort of sense to buy seven of Bournemouth's 1965 convertibles when newer models replaced them. But there wasn't a lot of similarity between 12-year-old DMO1-7 and the huge native DMS/DM class, beyond the fact that they had Daimler badges or had a model name beginning with the sixth letter of the alphabet and ending in the fifth.

The DMOs didn't last long with LT, but then neither did their more numerous Fleetline cousins, which were sold from 1979. That certainly didn't mark the end of the type in London, and the sightseeing market — deregulated from October 1980 — was well served by DMSs sold through the rapidly-expanding Ensign dealership. Some went to LT's competitors, others to companies sub-contracted

Marketing hadn't entered the bus industry lexicon in the early 1980s, when a bland all-over-white livery was deemed good enough to attract holidaymakers onto this Leyland Atlantean being operated in Weston-super-Mare by the Bristol Omnibus Co. It had been new to Maidstone & District in 1963 and was bought by Bristol in 1980, when its Weymann body was converted to open-top. Stewart J. Brown

to run the Round London Sightseeing Tour. Ensign hired buses to LT and also had a stake in London Pride, a tour business set up by Leon Daniels after Prince Marshall's death. Increasing numbers of DMSs were converted to open-top and ran alongside an array of other types that included converted Northern General Routemasters, an ex-Morecambe AEC Regent III and several Bristol VRTs.

The market was shaken up further in 1983 when Culturebus started up, using covered-top DMSs to provide a hop-on, hop-off tourist bus service linking the capital's main attractions. Although it didn't succeed in any of its forms, Culturebus did move the London bus tour market away from the idea that you were trapped aboard for two hours. For a time, Culturebus was an Ensign company.

By 1986 LT was more confident that the Routemaster's days were ending and transferred 50 into its newly formed London Coaches division to run the sightseeing tour. The idea was that it then had a piece of hardware — a traditional half-cab double-decker — that none of its competitors possessed, and many of these were rebuilt either as open-toppers or as convertibles with removable roofs. The downside of using half-cabs was that, unlike the DMSs or, indeed, the original D9s, this mixture of standard RMs and former Green Line RCLs had only 36 seats upstairs. In 1990 London

Coaches found a novel way round the problem by inserting a single bay from scrap Routemasters into 10 RMs, thus lengthening them to create 32ft 6in ERMs. Total seating capacity went up from 64 to 76, but the critical figure was upstairs, where there now were 44 seats for sale. The fact that their extra 5ft length was all in the wheelbase — and that manoeuvrability was on a par with an ocean-going supertanker — was another matter altogether.

The development of open-top sightseeing tours across much of the rest of Britain was due largely to the endeavours of one Cornishman and the company he founded around the time that London Transport was hiring in its D9s. The Cornishman was Roger Thompson, and his company became Guide Friday.

Thompson wasn't a busman by design but a tourism professional who discovered that second-hand buses would deliver a tourist product. His parents ran a guest house in Padstow for 35 years and, after attending public school, he found himself working increasingly in or around the Cornish hotel trade. For a time he owned a hotel, putting his energy and personality into developing the bar

Left: 'Sir Francis Drake' illustrates Devon General's 'Sea Dog' Atlanteans, albeit in NBC days and in poppy red and white rather than in its original Devon General cream and maroon. New in 1961, 'Sir Francis' is seen at the Derby — always a draw for open-top buses — in 1973. *Stewart J. Brown*

Below left: There was a time when the idea of open-top tours in Scotland would have seemed laughable. Aberdeen Corporation operated city tours using closed-top double-deckers, complete with public address, so the move to open-toppers by its successor was perhaps a logical one. In 2001, when this bus was photographed, First Aberdeen had four Alexander-bodied Atlanteans running as open-toppers. This one dated from 1980; the oldest was a 1978 bus. *Stewart J. Brown*

Above: Even places as damp as the Lake District can support open-top buses. A 1981 Stagecoach Titan, newly transferred from the group's London operations to a quieter life in the Lakes, waits for customers at Windermere railway station in 2001. *Stewart J. Brown*

Left: For a short time, some London sightseeing buses had offside doors, to provide for safer passenger movements at locations where it made more sense to stop at the right-hand kerb. The unusual-looking result is illustrated by a London Pride Dennis Dominator — never a common type in the capital — with Northern Counties body. *Stewart J. Brown*

Below: Fitting a large number of bus seats on the top deck and removing the roof turned 12m-long MCW Metroliners into ideal London sightseeing buses, even if crawling round the capital's congested streets was as far removed from the Metroliner's original purpose as can be imagined. *Stewart J. Brown*

and restaurant side before realising that financial stability lay in some sort of year-round business.

Thompson's plan was to move to London and become a lawyer, but tour-guiding held more attraction, and he was soon driving small parties of American tourists round Britain by car — a business he would later call Guide Friday. With the National Exhibition Centre being built on its doorstep, he reckoned that Stratford-upon-Avon would provide new opportunities for his business, and that was how, almost accidentally, he got into running buses. He discovered that Shakespeare's birthplace — one of the top destinations for foreign visitors touring Britain — undersold itself grossly. Coaches called in on their round-Britain tours, but there wasn't any bus tour of the town.

Thompson launched what initially was called Stratford-go-Round, using a 20-seat Bedford coach — 'of dubious age', as he once told me — to take visitors on an in-depth tour of the attractions in and around the town. It worked reasonably well in the hot summer of 1976 and again in 1977, the year of HM The Queen's Silver Jubilee, but a subsequent collapse in demand prompted him to rethink what Guide Friday should do.

As a marketeer rather than a busman, Thompson recognised that, although Stratford-go-Round was what he wanted his customers to appreciate, it wasn't what the market wanted. While he could sometimes fill a 20-seater with people prepared to spend half a day riding between — and experiencing guided tours of — the key Shakespearian sights, research showed that more people wanted something else. They wanted a bus tour that gave them access to the various properties when they wanted to visit them. They could choose to ride the whole route in one go, or stop off at some or all of the attractions for as long as they wished.

Thompson battled through the traffic courts to get a licence and, without any preconceptions of what he needed, went out and bought an ex-Leicester Leyland PD3, had it converted to open-top and started his first hop-on, hop-off tour, with professional guides providing an entertaining commentary in English. He also soon realised that, quaint and traditional as they might indeed be, half-cabs were not as well suited to the work as were rear-engined Atlanteans and Fleetlines (many of which were duly bought from Nottingham City Transport); apart from the crucial top-deck capacity, there also was the issue of fare collection. On the likes of an Atlantean the driver handled all that side of the business and supervised boarding and alighting while the guide concentrated on providing the information and entertainment.

It took the best part of 10 years for Guide Friday to break out of Stratford, but expansion then came rapidly as it moved into the other main tourist destinations, starting in Cambridge in 1988, Edinburgh in 1989, then Oxford, Bath and York. Soon, these cities — which previously had few (if any) open-top tours — boasted all-year tours, and, although Guide Friday often put a covered-top bus in for the winter, the market soon proved that it was willing to ride on open-toppers in all weathers. This was a far hardier market than the traditional seaside one.

In Edinburgh, Guide Friday also hooked passengers into its tours by running a bus service from the city's airport, and this greatly upset the city's main operator, which has seldom taken kindly to competitors. Having believed until 1989 that open-toppers wouldn't work so far north, Lothian, which had long run half-day coach and bus tours of the Scottish capital, was soon stung into action and cut the roofs off some of its own Atlanteans. Not content at that, it struck back at Guide Friday and set up its own competing ventures — Classic Tours — in Oxford, York and Cambridge. The last of these, in Oxford, didn't close until 2002.

In York and Bath, there was a substantial volume of competition, with several operators running open-toppers of varying standard, and such were the numbers of old double-deckers running round the Georgian city of Bath that residents of the Royal Crescent campaigned to ban buses from their prestigious address.

Guide Friday itself went on growing, acquiring other operators' tours in other places — like Windsor and Glasgow — and establishing shorter-season tours in places like Birmingham and Dundee — even in traditional open-top country like Brighton. There were setbacks too. Salisbury and Canterbury were too small to sustain its typical tours, the situation in Canterbury made worse because there aren't enough hotels to keep visitors there overnight.

One of Guide Friday's biggest failures was in the Lake District, where it underestimated the strength and ambition of the established operator. It set up a Windermere tour in 1990, imagining that Cumberland Motor Services (by then owned by Stagecoach) was as focused on local bus operations as established operators were in other places where Guide Friday had set up shop. But Stagecoach wasn't like other operators then, and the summer leisure market was essential for Cumberland's prosperity. By now it also owned Southdown, which still had those convertible VRs that NBC had most helpfully bought a dozen years before, and some of these were drafted quickly into

Windermere and painted in an apple-green-and-cream livery that was not only similar to traditional Southdown colours but also a bit like Guide Friday's darker green and cream. Stagecoach won the battle and still runs apple-green-and-cream open-toppers through the South Lakes today — even if Titans and Olympians have replaced the VRs.

Elsewhere, Guide Friday eschewed confrontation and often garaged its buses on the premises of established operators. Quite often, the established operators staffed and sometimes owned the buses run in Guide Friday colours. And, just to prove that Windermere bygones were also bygones in Stratford and Perth, Stagecoach operated Guide Friday tours in both Perth and Inverness. In its own right, Stagecoach has introduced open-toppers to such hitherto unlikely locations as Dunoon and the islands of Arran and Bute on the Firth of Clyde.

The one big place Guide Friday never cracked was London. It came close in 1992, when it was named as preferred bidder to buy London Coaches, the first part of London Buses to be privatised. Roger Thompson pulled out when he had a closer look at the books and at the way the business operated. The market was more competitive than anywhere else in Britain, and the still-large fleet of Routemasters didn't fit with the Guide Friday model. Instead, the London Coaches management team got the company and soon replaced most of the Routemasters with rear-engined double-deckers, including 12m Metroliner motorway coaches converted to open-top with over 50 seats for sale. Arriva bought the sightseeing part of the business in 1998.

Guide Friday began expanding into Continental Europe in 1991 and also into Ireland, starting with joint ventures in Seville and Paris and using brand-new buses in the French capital. But the business suffered a cruel blow when Roger Thompson, still only 55, died in 1996. Although the business carried on trading, the driving force had gone, and it was in a weak position when a determined new rival appeared on the scene four years later.

The new rival had been involved in the business since London Transport hired its D9s. City Sightseeing was run by Ensign's Peter Newman and his two sons, and was determined to become a global brand in the sightseeing bus market. It began putting together a patchwork of directly-operated and franchised tours in Britain and abroad, with buses painted in an eye-catching bright-red livery with graphics designed for each of the tour locations. Many of these tours were operated using four- and six-wheel Metrobuses from the Ensign dealership. Among its most significant early moves was to reacquire London Pride, which Ensign had

sold in 1998, and sell it on a little later to Arriva, which now runs some of its Original London Sightseeing Tour buses under the City Sightseeing franchise. Consolidation has left Arriva and The Big Bus Company (another company founded in the 1980s) as London's main open-top tour-bus companies.

By linking up with several of its rivals in places like York, Bath and Edinburgh, City Sightseeing was soon competing directly with Guide Friday, generally offering taped commentaries (sometimes in several languages) against Guide Friday's live guides. Lothian took on the franchise for Edinburgh and applied the red livery to four brand-new Dennis Trident open-toppers — the first new all-year open-top buses built for any British fleet since before World War 2.

City Sightseeing also set up in Cambridge and — leaving no doubt that it meant business — in Stratford, where it broke Guide Friday's dominance in 2001 by taking over the defunct Stratford Blue bus company. By then the writing was on the wall for Guide Friday, and it finally sold out to Ensign in May 2002. Rationalisation followed over the summer months, with some Guide Friday operations being sold to City Sightseeing franchisees, and the green buses disappeared quite rapidly from Stratford. Most of the elderly Atlanteans and Fleetlines (including one of the ex-London DMOs new to Bournemouth in 1965) went even quicker. Between them, the two companies had accumulated over 260 buses at around 30 locations — not bad, when you consider how rare open-toppers were 30 years ago.

For all that, and although there are far fewer than 30 years ago, the seaside open-topper isn't yet dead. As successor to Southdown, Brighton & Hove bought two convertible Dennis Tridents in 1999 and ordered similar East Lancs bodies on two Scania OmniDekkas due in 2003. Yellow Buses took three Volvo B7TL/East Lancs convertibles for Bournemouth in 2002. Neighbouring Wilts & Dorset had five relatively modern Northern Counties Palatine II-bodied DAF DB250s rebuilt as convertibles for its Bournemouth-area routes, and, to replace the VRs that had themselves replaced Devon General's 'Sea Dog' Atlanteans, Stagecoach Devon had a similar job done on six Alexander-bodied Scania N113s cascaded from London.

But, had it not been for the inspirational pioneering work of Obsolete Fleet and Guide Friday nearly 30 years ago, open-toppers would be rare indeed, and an important source of income would have been lost to the bus industry. Their contribution should not be forgotten.

Left: Lothian Region Transport set up operations in Oxford, Cambridge and York. A 1973 Alexander-bodied Atlantean is seen in Oxford in 2001. *Stewart J. Brown*

Below: A Routemaster in the Big Bus Company fleet negotiates Marble Arch in 1993, with hardy tourists determined to enjoy the early spring sunshine. This bus was new to Northern General in 1965 and was one of a small number of Northern General Routemasters to see further use on London tour operations after being withdrawn from service in northeast England in the late 1970s. *Stewart J. Brown*

Above right: What started life as London Transport's Round London Sightseeing Tour is now operated by Arriva as The Original Tour. Its oldest buses are Routemasters; the next-oldest are 1979 Titans and Metrobuses. This Metrobus was transferred from Arriva's London bus operations in 1999. *Stewart J. Brown*

Below right: A stretched Routemaster in the London Coaches fleet — type code ERM (for Extended) — passes through Trafalgar Square. The added length increased top-deck seating capacity by 10%, from 40 to 44. *Stewart J. Brown*

SAVE THE LAST DART FOR ME

Today's new buses are tomorrow's candidates for preservation. Gavin Booth, editor of *Classic Bus*, wonders which of the buses currently running on British streets ought to be kept for posterity.

All photographs by the author

Just imagine – the bus preservation movement in the UK has largely collapsed because there are so few youngsters coming along with an interest in buses. The older generation of preservationists still survive, of course, preserving the buses of their childhood, but there is no interest in anything newer than 20 years old.

Impossible? I hope so, but many preservation groups are bemoaning the lack of younger recruits, and nationwide organisations like the Omnibus Society and the PSV Circle are aware of an ageing membership.

But just suppose for a few moments that bus preservation faces this scenario. It's fair to say that,

if the number of additions to the preserved bus population started to slow down, there wouldn't be a total lack of preserved buses. There are literally thousands of them around the UK in museums, sheds, farms, bus garages, back gardens, and the realisation that ordinary individuals, using a combination of skill, money, luck and downright determination, could actually tackle the restoration of a full-size bus has meant that today's preserved bus fleet has grown to its present size from a handful of known preserved buses some 40 years ago.

Some of you may remember my first book, *Bus Stop*, an anthology of buses published by Ian Allan Ltd in 1969. In this I contributed an article suggesting what the 'vintage' buses of the 1990s might be. At that time the 1990s seemed an eternity away — good grief, we hadn't yet reached the 1970s!

In 1969 it would not have been difficult to jot down details of most of the known preserved buses in the UK, not because we had good memories but because there were so few of them. For a start, preservationists were still concentrating on older buses, which usually meant the prewar vehicles that were known to survive around the country. Representative examples of much of the postwar fleet were still around, often in service, so there didn't seem to be any rush to preserve them.

It was the big, well-funded organisations that had taken the lead in bus preservation. In 1969 the London Transport and British Transport Commission collections were housed in the Museum of British Transport at Clapham, London,

and both (but LT in particular) had adopted a very far-seeing approach to the preservation of not just their buses, trams, trolleybuses and trains but also artefacts of all sizes.

My *Bus Stop* article was written well before the preservation boom of the 1970s and imagined the types that should be preserved if a truly representative selection of UK buses were to remain for future generations to enjoy. At that time it seemed likely that we would be lucky to have just one representative of the types nominated; in practice there are, without exception, several, even dozens; some London types even reach three figures.

In 1969 I hoped there would be London RFs, Routemasters and 'even Red Arrows'; today the invaluable PSV Circle publication *Preserved Buses* lists 79 preserved RF-type AEC Regal IVs as well as 27 of the 84 GS-type Guy Specials — nearly one third of that fleet. Red Arrows? Yes, some of them — and as for RTs and RMs, I didn't even start to count them, as I had an editorial deadline to meet.

Outside London I hoped at least one Bristol LS, MW and Lodekka would survive; it's safe to say they did. A BET-style 36ft bus? Yes. The MCW Orion? Of course. A Harrington Cavalier coach? No problem — and so it goes on. It may not seem

Left: **In the days when enthusiasts knew virtually every preserved bus, 1929 all-Leyland Titan TD1 DR 4902 at the Museum of British Transport at Clapham in the mid-1960s.**

Below: **The 260 ECW-bodied Leyland Olympians bought by London Buses in 1986/7 were significant as the last big centralised order for double-deckers for London.**

Above: **Many of London's earliest Dennis Darts have been cascaded to fleets around the country. A 1990 bus with Carlyle Dartline body is seen after transfer to Stagecoach Devon.**

Left: **The Wright Handy-bus body gave some early Darts a distinctive — almost retro — look. A Westlink example is seen at Surbiton.**

Above right: **The Dennis Dart SLF/Plaxton Pointer has become a staple for London operators. A 10.1m-long London United bus is seen when new in 2001 on Kingston Bridge.**

Right: **First's London fleet includes a substantial number of Dennis Dart SLFs with Marshall Capital bodies. One is seen at Golders Green in August 2001.**

like amazing foresight now — and probably wasn't, even in 1969 — but there was no way of knowing just how preservation would take off. But at least today I can say that one example — minimum — of every type I suggested has survived.

But back to my original hypothesis. What if the enthusiasm runs out and we are back to ensuring that at least one representative of major types survives? What should be saved of the fleet currently operating on the UK roads?

London is maybe the obvious place to start, but with ownership of the vehicles passing from London Buses to individual contractors, will there be the same considered approach to preservation by Transport for London? Obviously we hope so, but look at how varied the fleet was in the 1980s and 1990s. From the post-Metrobus/Titan generation, what's worth keeping?

Start with double-deckers, though it's worth remembering that the London double-deck fleet dropped from 5,585 in 1980 to 4,157 in 2001 — or from 86% of the 1980 fleet to 57% of the combined 2001 fleets. But remember that the 2001 London fleet was much larger — 7,337 buses against 6,481

— which means that single-deck totals have shot up. Nonetheless the London double-decker is still a force to be reckoned with — particularly if you're a bus builder – and London still represents by far the biggest UK market for double-deckers.

The last big delivery of double-deckers ordered by London Buses comprised the 260 Leyland Olympians with the final Eastern Coach Works bodies, placed in service in 1986/7. Although they are not too different from other buses built for London and, indeed, other parts of the country, they are significant because they were the last major London order before the break-up of London Buses into smaller units as a prelude to privatisation. So one of them would be appropriate.

Although there were fewer of them, one of the Volvo B10M double-deckers with Alexander R-type bodies bought in 1988 by Grey-Green would be important to save. These were used on the 24 route between Hampstead Heath and Pimlico, but most importantly they were extremely visible as they ran through Trafalgar Square, Whitehall and Parliament Square, being painted not in London red but in the operator's attractive grey/green/orange livery. This was the first Central London route awarded to a non-London Buses company, and the Grey-Green Volvos certainly stood out in a sea of red. No 80%-red rule then.

London's double-deck intake in the 1990s was increasingly dictated by what manufacturers could supply quickly from stock to meet contract requirements. Some reasonably-sized batches stand out from the crowd, notably Stagecoach's long Volvo Olympians with Alexander or Northern Counties bodies, or the Northern Counties-bodied Olympians for Kentish Bus, or the unusual Dennis Arrows for Capital Citybus, or perhaps the very late step-entry Volvo Olympian/Northern Counties bought in 1999 by First CentreWest. The list could go on, and doubtless London preservationists have their own ideas, but the variety of double-deckers and liveries in the 1990s certainly offered plenty of scope.

You might think that things have settled down more recently, now that we are in the low-floor double-deck era. After all, there are just four chassis currently available — the DAF DB250, Dennis Trident, Scania OmniDekka and Volvo B7TL — and just six builders producing bodies for them — East Lancs, Optare, TransBus Falkirk, Belfast and Wigan, and Wrightbus — so the choice is fairly limited. In fact the permutations are endless, particularly with a range of different lengths. In practice the big groups have stuck largely to their favoured types, so Arriva has bought DAF DB250s with Alexander or Plaxton bodywork, as well as Wright-bodied Volvo B7TLs; First has favoured Plaxton President- and Alexander ALX400-bodied Dennis Tridents; Go-Ahead has built up a substantial fleet of B7TL/Presidents for its London Central and London General fleets and also has some B7TLs with East Lancs Vyking or Wrightbus Eclipse Gemini bodies; Stagecoach in London favours Trident/ALX400s.

Other growing low-floor fleets in London are operated by Connex (Trident/ALX400), London United (B7TLs bodied by Alexander, Plaxton and Wrightbus) and Metroline (B7TL/Plaxton, Trident/Alexander and Trident/Plaxton). Future preservationists will argue about which of these deserve to be preserved, but significant buses could include one of the DAF DB250s that Arriva used to beat everyone else to operate the first low-floor double-deckers in London, or those very early DAFs, including the first production Plaxton Presidents, that went to Capital Logistics in 1999 for the ill-fated 60 route.

Typical London single-deckers of the past 15 years can be summed up in two words: Dennis Dart. There were 2,700 of them in service with London operators at the beginning of 2002, nearly 80% of them SLF low-floor examples. Older step-entry Darts flooded the London fleets from 1990, but many have been cascaded to other fleets around the country. Increasingly the Reeve Burgess (later Plaxton) Pointer body became the standard, though in a sometimes bewildering variety of lengths and door configurations. An early Duple Dart would seem to be a 'must', along with one of the distinctive retro-look Wright Handy-bus examples from the same period. Of the SLF Darts, one of the vast fleet of well over 1,000 Pointers would seem to be essential, as well as an Alexander ALX200 and one of the surprisingly large fleet of Marshall Capitals operating for First.

Big single-deckers have not been favoured much in London since Leyland National days, at least until fairly recently with the influx of rigid and articulated Mercedes-Benz Citaros. Perhaps the most significant full-size single-deckers of recent years were those pioneering low-floor buses bodied by Wright on Dennis Lance SLF and Scania N113CRL chassis in 1993/4. Then there are the 17 East Lancs Myllennium-bodied DAF SB220s bought in 1999 for services to the Dome at Greenwich. Although there were grand plans to run these on a dedicated busway, this never materialised, and, rather like the Dome itself, they never quite realised their full potential.

Minibuses have been playing a smaller role in London recently, but one of the MA-class Mercedes-Benz 811D/Alexanders bought 1988-91 would be appropriate, as these refined the concept of van-derived minibuses by offering a longer and more spacious bus. Otherwise there were, of course, MetroRiders a-plenty and those distinctive Optare CityPacers built on Volkswagen LT55 chassis, though a glance at *Preserved Buses* reveals that at least one of the CityPacers is already preserved.

In the rest of Britain things are arguably considerably simpler. The growth of the big groups in the 1990s has led not only to standardised buses but also to standardised liveries. Now, with nationwide fleet numbering as well, the once-complicated business of transferring buses between group companies has been reduced to a simple matter of changing the legal lettering and the local

Left: At Meadowhall in August 1995, a 1994 Volvo B10B with Alexander Strider bodywork in the West Riding fleet.

Below: In the days before FirstBus, Grampian was standardising on Mercedes-Benz O405 buses, in this case with Optare Prisma body. This is Union Street, Aberdeen, in August 1998 with an O405 in Park & Ride livery.

Right: In full 'Barbie' livery but without any company identification, a new Scania L113CRL with Axcess-floline body outside the Wright coachworks at Ballymena, ready for delivery to FirstGroup.

Below right: The Dennis Dart SLF/Plaxton Pointer has been popular with FirstGroup. This example, seen in Castlegate, Aberdeen, in August 1998, was new that year but in 2001 passed to First Badgerline.

fleetname, though First doesn't even have to do the latter. As a result, enthusiasts often bemoan the lack of variety as they travel around Britain. The First or Stagecoach buses in Town A are identical to those in Town B, they say, and are therefore boring. The 'high heid yins' (as we say in Scotland) at Aberdeen or Perth can, I'm sure, produce figures that show how much this is saving in paint, vinyls and labour, but the enthusiasts may remain unmoved by this argument.

Arriva has a less standardised fleet than those of First and Stagecoach, partly due to its later creation, which has meant that it has inherited a mixed selection of buses of all sizes. Inevitably it has Dennis Dart/Plaxton Pointers by the hundred, and, as Arriva Bus & Coach is the UK's DAF importer, there is a growing fleet of the midi-size SB120 chassis. DAFs are also represented in Arriva's double-deck fleet, including a number of East Lancs Lowlander-bodied DB250 low-floor double-deckers. A typical Arriva bus is harder to pinpoint, but one of the 92 DAF SB220/Plaxton Prestige low-floor single-deckers would be unusual, especially one of the LPG-powered examples. In its earlier existence as British Bus, the group bought East Lancs-bodied Scanias, including L113CRLs and low-floor MaxCis — both types readily associated with Arriva and its predecessors. Other distinctive types inherited from British Bus were the Alexander Strider-bodied Volvo B10Bs that were new to the West Riding and Yorkshire Woollen fleets under Caldaire ownership.

First's roots were in Badgerline and GRT Holdings — two groups that were developing distinctive vehicle policies. Badgerline favoured Dennis/Plaxton products, and most distinctive were the Verde-bodied Lances bought in the early 1990s. GRT went for unusual single-deckers too, including Mercedes-Benz O405s (with Optare or Wright bodywork) that would be representative of their era in the ranks of preservation.

When FirstBus was formed it started to buy the inevitable Dart/Pointer combination and has also built up a substantial fleet of full-size buses with Wright bodywork, first on Scania L113CRL and Volvo B10BLE chassis and currently on Scania L94UB and Volvo B7L. Any of these, in full 'Barbie' livery, would be appropriate to show future generations what a typical FirstGroup bus looked like. Less typical, but reflecting First thinking, would be one of the Volvo/Wright articulated buses, or perhaps Grampian's unique Alexander-bodied 1992 Mercedes-Benz O405G.

First's concentration on single-deckers has meant that, outside London, new double-deckers have been more limited, but the attractive Volvo Olympians with Alexander Royale or Northern Counties Palatine II bodies from the mid-1990s would be significant, and, although they are by no means representative, one of the 2002-delivered three-axle Volvo B7TLs with East Lancs Nordic bodies would certainly be different.

Stagecoach started on vehicle standardisation long before the other big groups — back in the late 1980s, with orders for long-wheelbase Leyland Olympians with Alexander RL-type bodywork — and Alexander has been favoured for many of its orders, on various types of Dennis Dart and Volvo B6 chassis, so representatives of these types would be significant. Alexander also bodied the three tri-axle Leyland Olympians, including the 110-seat 'Megadekka' — surely a preservation candidate. Very much a Stagecoach staple is the Volvo B10M/Alexander PS type, a sturdy and sensible bus that is found throughout its fleets. Another B10M type developed for Stagecoach has the Plaxton Interurban body, for express work. Stagecoach also bought articulated versions of the B10M with both Plaxton and Jonckheere bodies, and one of these would represent a phase in the group's vehicle development. Like First, Stagecoach concentrates most of its low-floor double-deckers in its London fleets but has also placed Dennis Tridents, mostly with Alexander ALX400 bodies, into its provincial fleets.

Beyond the big groups, we can go for types.

There will be no problem finding Plaxton Pointer Darts to preserve, as virtually every fleet in the country seems to have them. Volvo B6 variants are thinner on the ground but are still to be found in fairly healthy numbers. What has been particularly interesting in recent years is the number of smaller independents — companies that in the past would have been buying second-hand buses — that have invested in new buses like Dart/Pointers or Optare Solos, often with the incentive of a local authority contract (sometimes because the contract stipulates low-floor buses), and there are precious few of these on the second-hand market at the moment. So maybe I could nominate an independent's Dart/Pointer, possibly the smallest-size MPD version, or one of Optare's innovative Solo minibuses.

Bigger single-deckers have become a rarer breed outside the big groups, but full-size DAFs, Mercedes, Scanias and Volvos have been sold to a number of local-authority, independent or smaller group fleets, and a good representative of these would be worth keeping.

New double-deckers outside London are, in overall numbers, still a minority taste. There are some operators that have never deserted the double-decker, like Travel West Midlands, Lothian Buses, Nottingham City, Brighton & Hove and Wilts & Dorset, and it would be appropriate to see, say, a TWM Volvo B7TL/President, as well as a Lothian Trident/President, or a Nottingham or Brighton Trident/East Lancs Lolyne, or a Wilts & Dorset or Reading Buses Optare Spectra. And, of course, low-floor double-deckers are not confined to London or to these operators; just look at the independents that have invested in these in recent years.

The ever-growing preserved bus population in Britain will provide future generations with a glimpse of the buses that were operating in the 20th century – particularly the second half of that century. Pre-World War 2 buses are inevitably thinner on the ground, and really early motor buses can be counted on the fingers of not many hands. London's practice of saving representative buses from major

classes means that we can trace the development of the modern bus from the B type onwards, and, while London tended to make the running in those pioneering days, preservationists like Mike Sutcliffe have ensured that non-London buses are represented too.

Those for whom buses ceased to be interesting when the engine moved from the front may care little about Darts and B7TLs, but we owe it to the next generations to ensure that significant representatives of these types are around long after we are. Let's hope I am as wrong in this article as I was in *Bus Stop* 30-odd years ago.

The Volvo B10M with Alexander PS-type body became a Stagecoach standard in the 1990s. This example was new to Stagecoach Manchester in 1996 but soon passed via the group's Midland Red fleet to its South Wales operations.

DOUBLE-DECK
RENAISSANCE?

New low-floor models have rekindled interest in double-deckers. *Stewart J. Brown* considers what's available.

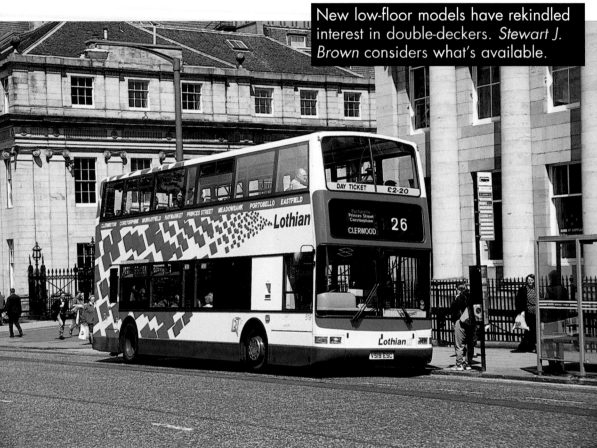

If there's one vehicle which has made a big impact on the British bus scene so far in the 21st century it's the low-floor double-decker. True, there are some areas where you'll struggle to find one — Merseyside, for example, and there are few anywhere north of Edinburgh — but where they are in evidence they have brought fresh new style to Britain's streets. They are also fully accessible, which, after all, is the reason they were developed — although that accessibility has come at some considerable cost in terms of the layout of the lower deck.

Double-deckers with step-free entrances are nothing new. They were around in the 1950s with

the Bristol Lodekka and Leyland Atlantean, although then the motivation was to reduce overall vehicle height rather than to improve access for the less-able members of the community.

The new generation of low-floor models has dramatically altered the fortunes of the manufacturers. Back in the 1990s the Volvo Olympian was king. The others — DAF, Dennis and Scania — were, let's be honest, also-rans. Scania had a few loyal customers, but it wasn't selling big volumes — although it did win some significant London orders in the early 1990s. DAF had a magnificent-looking product with the Optare Spectra, but there were few big fleets of them.

Left: **Lothian Buses operates Scotland's biggest fleet of low-floor double-deckers. Most are Dennis Tridents with Plaxton President bodies. Bonded glazing is specified.** *Stewart J. Brown*

Above: **Go North East operates Dennis Tridents with bodies by East Lancs and, on more recent deliveries, Plaxton. This is a 2001 Trident with 75-seat Plaxton President body.** *Stewart J. Brown*

Right: **East Yorkshire operates this Volvo B7TL with Plaxton President body, one of eight delivered in 2002.** *Volvo Bus*

Above: **The changing shape of the double-decker. Both these buses in the Blackpool Transport fleet have East Lancs bodies. The Dennis Trident with Lolyne bodywork nearest the camera was delivered in 2002. The new Tridents were replacing 1980 Atlanteans, such as the bus seen alongside.** *Stewart J. Brown*

Right: **The original new-generation East Lancs body had this style of front, with a two-piece double-curvature lower-deck windscreen. This is a Trident in the fleet of Mayne of Manchester.** *Stewart J. Brown*

The DAF chassis was also bodied by Northern Counties, but not in big numbers. Dennis's Dominator was dying, and its Arrow never really took flight. And then there was the Volvo Citybus, based on the B10M coach chassis — but that never found widespread popularity, although there were a few big users such as Strathclyde, London General and Grey-Green.

Today it's a very different story. Dennis — or TransBus, as it now prefers to be known — has ousted Volvo as Britain's leading double-deck supplier and has sold Tridents to fleets which wouldn't have considered buying a Dominator, let alone an Arrow. All of Stagecoach's low-floor double-deckers — approaching 800 — are Dennis Tridents. Indeed, when the Trident was announced in 1997 Stagecoach immediately ordered 100, which at the time was the biggest UK double-deck order ever placed with Dennis. Similarly Lothian Buses, a company which for the best part of 40 years bought little other than Leylands or Volvos (as Leyland's successor) for its bus fleet, now runs a low-floor double-deck fleet made up almost entirely of Dennises. It does have six Volvo B7TLs, but having settled on the Trident shows no sign of switching back to Volvo. In London, FirstGroup's standard double-decker is the Trident, although elsewhere it runs B7TLs, with the biggest concentration in its Yorkshire fleets, where there are almost 100. It also has a few Volvos in the

capital. Metroline, which had been an Olympian buyer, has divided its business between Dennis and Volvo.

The root cause of Volvo's trouble is that Dennis got there first. Volvo hoped to sell UK operators a double-deck version of the B7L single-decker, with the engine in the rear corner. UK operators with one voice said 'no'. Volvo went back to the drawing-board and produced the transverse-engined B7TL. Stable doors and bolting horses come to mind.

When the B7L/President was unveiled Volvo said it would enter trial service in London. It never did. Indeed, it never entered service anywhere. However, the B7TL is now securing respectable sales — it's the first choice of Go-Ahead in London and of London United (although both operators run some Tridents too) and is the Dublin Bus standard — but it seems unlikely that the B7TL will ever overtake the Trident.

In fact, Dennis didn't really get there first. DAF Bus did. DAF had a low-floor DB250 chassis at Coach & Bus '95 — that's almost 10 years ago — and the first of the current generation of low-floor double-deckers to enter service did so with ABus in Bristol in February 1998, narrowly beating Travel West Midlands, both operators running DAFs. It would be January 1999 before the first Dennis Trident entered service, with Stagecoach in London. The first Volvo B7TLs did not appear on the streets until October 1999. Those streets were in Birmingham. The operator was Travel West Midlands.

DAF Bus has benefited from its connections with Arriva, which has seen almost 500 DB250s enter service with Arriva's London companies. Most of these have been bodied by Alexander, but there are a few with Plaxton President bodies. London's first low-floor bus was an Arriva DAF/Alexander. However, outside London most modern Arriva double-deckers are Volvos, plus a few Dennises. There are, of course, Volvos in London too, with distinctive Wrightbus bodies. Elsewhere, though, low-floor DAFs are less common. There are none in Scotland or Wales. Outside London the main user is Wilts & Dorset, with Optare-bodied examples.

For a time it looked as though Scania might not pursue double-deck business in Britain, as it promoted its articulated L94UA as an alternative approach to high-capacity transport. However,

in 2002 it announced a new model, the N94UD OmniDekka. This uses a modified version of the N94 OmniCity underframe, with bodywork by East Lancs which incorporates some OmniCity styling for the front panel. This model quickly won orders from Metrobus and Brighton & Hove, both part of Go-Ahead Group, and from Nottingham City Transport. The first vehicles, for Metrobus, entered service early in 2003. Metrobus had previously bought Tridents, and was another operator which had standardised on Volvo Olympians in the 1990s.

The new range of chassis required a new approach from bodybuilders. For Optare there was a re-engineering of the Spectra body to produce a low-floor bus which to most casual observers looks little different from the original step-entrance model. It's a tribute to the quality of the original Spectra design — a trend-setter in its day — that it doesn't look out of place alongside the new bodies developed by other builders. The Spectra is built exclusively on the DAF Bus chassis.

Both Alexander and Plaxton (Northern Counties as was) had all-new designs at Coach & Bus '97, and these have continued little-changed.

Plaxton's body was the President, and it is available on the three leading chassis — DAF, Dennis and Volvo. In the early days most Presidents had bonded glazing, but more recently there has been a switch to gasket glazing, which may look less stylish but is cheaper to replace.

Left: **All of Wrightbus's initial successes with its Eclipse Gemini were in London, with orders from Arriva, Go-Ahead and London United, all on Volvo B7TL chassis. A London General example loads at South Kensington in 2002.** *Stewart J. Brown*

Below: **London United has just three Wrightbus double-deckers; most of its recent double-deckers have been bodied by Alexander. The VR-series fleetnumber is redolent of a previous generation of double-decker.** *Volvo Bus*

Above: **Blazefield operates coach-seated Presidents in two of its fleets — Yorkshire Coastliner and Burnley & Pendle. These are based on Volvo chassis and are used for inter-urban limited-stop services. The single-piece upper-deck windscreen is an option on the President.** *TransBus*

Left: **To demonstrate its new model, Wrightbus produced this vehicle in 2001, based on a long-wheelbase B7TL chassis and incorporating bonded glazing. It is seen in Falkirk — coincidentally the home of one of TransBus's plants — in the company of a Wright-bodied single-decker operated by FirstGroup. What looks like a handrail on the front nearside corner of the upper deck is a device to keep low branches clear of the windscreen.** *Wrightbus*

A low-height version of the President has been built on Dennis Trident chassis, the only examples so far being seven for Stagecoach in Cambridge, delivered in 2000.

The Alexander ALX400, like the President, is offered on the same three chassis. It has square-cornered gasket glazing, which in style terms offers something approaching the crisp appearance provided by bonded glass while in maintenance terms avoids the higher replacement costs for damaged windows.

When the ALX400 and the President were launched they were head-to-head competitors. That has all changed with the creation in 2001 of TransBus, and both form part of the TransBus range, although rationalisation must surely come, perhaps in the shape of an Enviro 400. The President is built at Wigan, the ALX400 at Falkirk and Belfast. Interesting among the Belfast plant's output have been bodies on Volvo B7TLs for Ulsterbus.

East Lancs developed a new line for the new chassis, and these are among the most attractive bodies to come out of the company's Blackburn factory for many years. The same basic body is offered on the Trident as the Lolyne and on the Volvo as the Vyking. It appeared in 2001 with a revised front — not universally greeted as an improvement — on the DAF as the Lowlander, for which the main customers have been Arriva and

Isle of Man Transport. The revised front was made available as an option on the Lolyne and the Vyking in 2002. With the Vyking East Lancs secured double-deck business in London, delivering a batch to London General in 2002.

The East Lancs family was extended to the new Scania in 2002, giving the company a broader spread of chassis than any of its competitors. An unusual feature of the Scania OmniDekka is the use of slightly shallower windows on the lower deck than on the upper deck; previously when different depths of windows have been used on double-deck bodies in Britain it's been the other way round, with shallower windows on the upper saloon.

Also in 2002 East Lancs built a batch of 10 tri-axle double-deckers for First Glasgow, using its Nordic body, developed for service in Copenhagen. These were based on the single-deck B7L chassis — the model which Volvo had wanted to sell in the UK back in 1997 — and were 12m-long air-conditioned 95-seaters.

In 2001 there appeared on the scene a new bodybuilder — Wrightbus. The Ballymena-based company had established a growing presence with its attractive single-deck bodies, and at Coach & Bus '99 stole the show with its 'next generation' Solar and Eclipse. The company's new double-decker picked up on that styling with its distinctively-shaped single-piece windscreen and was launched on the Volvo B7TL as the Eclipse

Below left: **Metroline operates both Volvos and Dennises with Plaxton President bodies. This bus, at Golders Green, is a 2002 Dennis Trident with gasket glazing. Metroline's original Presidents had bonded windows.** *Stewart J. Brown*

Above: **The Dennis Trident is Britain's most common low-floor double-decker, and Stagecoach was one of the first customers for the model. Most of Stagecoach's Tridents are in London and have Alexander ALX400 bodies. One of the first Tridents is seen posed with one of the last of the previous generation of Stagecoach double-deckers, an Alexander-bodied Volvo Olympian.** *Stewart J. Brown*

Gemini, the name being a play on the zodiac sign for twins on a body with two decks. The first customer was Arriva London, which was quickly followed by Go-Ahead London. The first order for Eclipse Geminis outside the capital came from Travel West Midlands, which took 60 in 2003. Also in 2003 Wrightbus announced that it would be bodying the DAF DB250 — presumably to satisfy Arriva.

The creation of TransBus could have interesting repercussions in double-deck sales. TransBus can supply a complete double-decker — a Trident with ALX400 or President bodywork — and also makes its Trident chassis available to one independent bodybuilder, East Lancs. It seems unlikely that the other independent builder of double-deckers, Wrightbus, will engineer its body to fit the TransBus chassis. Equally, TransBus provides bodywork on chassis of other manufacturers — DAF Bus and

Volvo — and most DAF and Volvo double-deckers do indeed have TransBus bodywork, although Wrightbus is winning business at TransBus's expense. The move by DAF to have Wrightbus body its DB250 chassis also has to be viewed against the background of developments at Optare.

The entire Optare range has gradually switched from being bodies on chassis to being integral products, with the exception of the DAF-based Spectra. Optare is developing a new integral double-decker. In the long term, can there be room for competing double-deck models — one integral, one chassis-based — coming from the Optare factory?

It's an exciting time for double-deckers, the only downside being that most of the excitement is in London. There are big fleets of low-floor double-deckers in Birmingham, Edinburgh, parts of West Yorkshire and parts of Greater Manchester, and you can find them in other places if you know where to look. Users other than those mentioned so far include Go North East, East Yorkshire, Newport Transport, First Hampshire, First Leicester, Southern Vectis, Bournemouth Transport, Yorkshire Traction, Strathtay, Ipswich Buses and Reading Transport. And there are also small numbers in small fleets, such as Mayne's of Manchester, Sergeant's of Kington and UK North of Manchester. Yet outside the capital it's hard not to conclude that the great days of the double-decker may be over. But people have said that many times before, and been proved wrong. I hope I'm wrong too.

Left: **Outside London, Travel West Midlands has been the biggest buyer of low-floor double-deckers. This one, seen in central Birmingham in 2000, is a Plaxton-bodied Volvo.** *Stewart J. Brown*

Below left: **Wilts & Dorset is a long-standing Optare customer. A low-floor Spectra, based on a DAF DB250 chassis, is seen in Salisbury.** *Stewart J. Brown*

Right: **A surprising number of small operators have added low-floor double-deckers to their fleets. These include UK North in Manchester. This is a DAF DB250 with Alexander ALX400 body.** *Stewart J. Brown*

Below: **The generous window sizes of the East Lancs Lolyne body are clearly seen on this Bournemouth Transport Trident. The four equal-sized side windows on the upper deck contrast with the products of other builders, which not only have more windows but use windows of various sizes.** *Stewart J. Brown*

BACKING A WINNER

Stephen Morris looks at the meteoric growth of his local bus operator, a company which has expanded to become a major presence in northwest Surrey and southwest London.

I have in my possession the invaluable LOTS *Buses of London Fleetbook* for 1994. 'So what?' you may say. So — it tells me that Tellings-Golden Miller had just one service bus, an unusual Caetano Stagecoach-bodied Volvo B10M 57-seater. 'This bus is used on 606', it states, this being the remnant of what had been a slightly larger network of local services on the borders of London and that bit of northwest Surrey which had once been Middlesex.

Things are a bit different now. Tellings-Golden Miller is a major force in southwest London and quite a large swathe of Surrey, not just the northwest corner, and, nine years after that book was published, had 163 service buses. Historically a 'bit player' in that strange hinterland between London Transport's red buses and green buses, it is now more than twice the size of the remains of what were London Transport's green buses in the area, now Arriva Guildford & West Surrey, though much of the fleet is used on what were once red bus routes. Indeed, its Dennis Darts run, amongst other things, a service which only 15 years ago was the furthest-flung outpost of the Routemaster in southwest London — at that time the 237 and now the 235.

The Bedfont service was started in 1955 by West London Coachways. A Bedford OB is seen at the official start of the service. *Ian Allan Library*

The horse that started it all: Golden Miller, 1930s racehorse extraordinaire, peers out through a lucky horseshoe from the back of one of Tellings-Golden Miller's latest Mini Pointer Darts. *Stephen Morris*

Tellings-Golden Miller's history dates back to 1923, when F. G. Wilder had started as a haulier. He was to buy his first coach — a Bedford OB — 32 years later, and then took over another local coach business, Varney of Twickenham, which traded as Golden Miller, named after a record-breaking racehorse of the 1930s. That Golden Miller, foaled in 1927 and named after his parents, Golden Court and Miller's Pride, won the Cheltenham Gold Cup every year from 1932 to 1936 and achieved a unique double in 1934 by winning the Grand National as well.

As a bus operator, Golden Miller dates back to 3 March 1967, when F. G. Wilder & Sons Ltd took over a local service between Feltham station and Bedfont. The concept of a local bus service operated by an independent operator within London Transport's tightly-controlled monopoly was almost unheard of at the time, but this little route, barely a mile long, had been started by West London Coachways on 7 October 1955. Following the retirement of one of West London's directors, the service was continued by his colleague, G. T. Mash, who ran Tourist Coachways Ltd of Hounslow. When Wilder took it over, London Transport was taking a slightly more relaxed view of independent operators running services in outlying parts of its empire; at around the same time, Elms Coaches took over the 98B and Isleworth Coaches took over Richmond-area route 235 — not to be confused with today's 235.

Golden Miller bought a Saro-bodied Leyland Tiger Cub (ORR 345) from East Midland to operate its new service, which obviously filled a need, and went on to start two further bus services less than a year later. A small terminus had been built alongside Feltham station; John Gillham, writing in *Buses Illustrated* in August 1967, describes it as 'large enough to hold at least six buses and … equipped with a large shelter, a prominent notice board and an attractive flower garden cultivated by Mr Mash' — a far cry from today's Feltham Interchange (though, while Golden Miller's services flourished like Mr Mash's flower garden, the same cannot be said of the T1-3 and T4 services to Heathrow for which the new and rather more functional interchange would be built in the 1990s).

Above: A typical Golden Miller bus of the 1970s, on the Bedfont service, which had by now become the 601. Three identical Bedfords were used, but this bus was more unusual — a prototype Bristol LH chassis with a Plaxton Derwent body. *Ian Allan Library*

Left: Golden Miller was the first independent to buy the Bristol LH, with a batch of six Plaxton-bodied coaches. This LH was driven to victory at the 1969 Brighton Coach Rally by James Griffiths, Coach Driver of the Year. *S. W. Stevens-Stratten*

Right: **Two of the Plaxton Derwent-bodied Bedford YRQs, at Feltham station on their first day.** *Ian Allan Library*

Left: **Golden Miller was also a pioneer in taking the first Volvo B58s for a British operator; one of the first coaches, with Duple Dominant bodywork, is seen here.** *Ian Allan Library*

Right: **Routes 601-3 passed to Fountain Coaches, running from Golden Miller's former premises in Fern Grove, Feltham. An unusual but regular performer on the 602 from Feltham to Shepperton, where it terminated outside the Ian Allan offices, was this TAZ Dubrava.** *Chris Leigh*

Right: **Merger in evidence: with 'Tellings of Weybridge' windscreen sticker and Tellings-Golden Miller fleetnames is a Jonckheere Jubilee P599-bodied Volvo B10M at Victoria.** *Chris Drew*

Right: Bus services all but disappeared after the merger; only this unusual Caetano Stagecoach-bodied Volvo B10M was kept, and just the Staines–Stanwell Moor route 606. The Stagecoach was quite useful for short private hires as well as bus use. *Michael Dryhurst*

Right: During its time as a Drawlane subsidiary Tellings-Golden Miller expanded and took over Globeheath of Cardiff. When Steve Telling bought back the business he kept the Cardiff premises and set up Cardiff Bluebird, in competition with Cardiff Bus. In the true spirit of deregulation a Cardiff Buebird MCW Metrorider prepares to race a newer Cardiff Bus Optare MetroRider away from the lights. *Stephen Morris*

The new services ran to Shepperton station, as the 602, and to Hanworth as the 603, while the Bedfont service was numbered 601. An ex-Northern General Albion Aberdonian was added to the fleet to cater for the increased demand. Walton-on-Thames Motor Co's service from Walton station to the town was taken over as the 604 in October 1970, and then on 1 September 1971 another new service was started, the 606 from Staines to Stanwell, extended in the peaks to Stanwell Moor.

A mixture of buses bought new and secondhand was used on these services, with a number of used Bristols, including an ex-Western National LS and an ex-Thames Valley full-front LWL, as well as a 1969 Bristol LH6L prototype chassis which, although intended to be bodied by Strachans, was eventually fitted with a Plaxton Derwent bus body. This had three-plus-two seating and used farebox operation, using the 'GM Farebox', to Golden Miller's own design. Indeed, Golden Miller was something of a pioneer in being the first independent operator to have Bristol LHs; six LH coaches were ordered in 1967 and delivered the following year. Three Bedford YLQ buses, also with Plaxton Derwent bodywork, followed in 1974, with a standee area to increase capacity. Second-hand acquisitions included a Ribble Leyland Leopard, a pair of ex-Manchester Panther Cubs and, towards the end, an ex-Aberdeen AEC Swift which was to prolong Swift operation in the area after both London Country and London Transport had disposed of theirs.

The other branch of the company, Tellings, is a rather more recent development. In 1972 one Steve Telling and his wife Christine, from Weybridge, bought a Duple Bella Ventura-bodied Bedford VAM, MYN 597D, new to local operator Ben Stanley of Hersham, for £2,750. In 1978 he moved to new premises on a garage forecourt in Byfleet and the following year bought his first new vehicles, a pair of Bedfords. With a fleet of three full-size coaches and two minibuses he moved to Wintersells Road, close to the old Brooklands race track in Byfleet.

Golden Miller had again been a pioneer in the 1970s, by buying the first Volvo B58s for a British operator (it'll never catch on, you know) and also bought DAF coaches well in advance of most other operators. In view of subsequent history it is perhaps paradoxical that Tellings' first Volvo, bought in 1980, was a Duple Dominant-bodied B58 (RHX 190L) bought from Golden Miller, and it was Volvo all the way then for this operator, which rapidly raised its profile during the 1980s and used an unmissable livery of mauve, yellow and white.

Some expansion took place, with the takeover of Jubilee Coaches of Chertsey in 1979, but Tellings was pipped at the post when it tried to buy Ben Stanley of Hersham. Some vehicles had even been repainted in Tellings' livery before the sale was thwarted. By now Tellings was running 10 coaches, and on 14 December 1984 it bought Golden Miller, which also had 10 coaches plus five service buses. The two businesses were run separately until the following August, when the Golden Miller fleet was moved from Fern Grove, Feltham, to Byfleet. Tellings-Golden Miller had been formed.

Steve Telling was not particularly enthusiastic about bus operation, and most of the services had passed their peak. The 604 had gone in 1974 — London Transport 218 being diverted to serve Walton station — and the 601 and 603 were passed to Fountain Coaches, which was running from Golden Miller's former Fern Grove premises in Feltham. They were amalgamated by Fountain to form the 600. The 602 was retained for the time being but cut back to a peak-hour operation. Only the 606 — Golden Miller's best route by some margin — was retained, the 602 also passing to Fountain Coaches. Meanwhile, a new and very unusual Caetano Stagecoach-bodied Volvo B10M was bought for the 606. Another followed, with an automatic gearbox, but lasted only a couple of years in the fleet before being sold to Hutchisons of Overtown.

Steve Telling was more interested in coach operation and modernised and expanded the combined coach fleet with 25 new Van Hool-bodied Volvo B10Ms delivered 1985-7. It looked like the dawning of a golden age for the coach business, and during 1988 agreement was reached with Glenton Tours, one of the most prestigious names in London coaching, that Glenton would dispose of its own fleet and use TGM's coaches from the following year. Twelve new vehicles were added for this work. However, not all was well as it appeared; despite its highly illustrious past, Glenton

Tours collapsed, as did two other tour operators for which Tellings-Golden Miller did work. Thus in 1990 Steve Telling decided to sell his business, to Midland Fox, and as a result found himself working for Drawlane.

More expansion came in the Drawlane era, which would see the Tellings-Golden Miller name appear in a variety of locations. First came Richmond-based Sheenway Coaches, which was amalgamated with the Byfleet business. Then, in April 1991, Globeheath of Cardiff was acquired; this company had been formed out of the old CK Tours operation, which had gained some notoriety for its competition with Cardiff City Transport in 1981/2 (before full deregulation) and now traded as the Coach Travel Centre. Two operators in Nuneaton were also acquired during this period.

Meanwhile, as the London Transport tendering process was giving operators around London more opportunity to develop into new areas of work, it seemed inevitable that Tellings-Golden Miller would enter the London Transport service scene. In 1991 the tenders were won for two services close to TGM's heartland, the 116 and 117 (Bedfont/Staines –Brentford), on the basis of using 12 refurbished Leyland Nationals, which were to be provided by Drawlane.

Drawlane already had two other subsidiaries in the area, London & Country and Speedlink Airport Services, which ran out of the old London Country garage at Staines, and the 116/117 operation was put into Staines too. The 'refurbished' Leyland Nationals were not quite as thoroughly modernised as they might have been; while some attention had been paid to sprucing up the interiors, that was as far as it went, and a blue-and-white livery, with 'TGM Buses' fleetnames, was used. The lack of attention that had been paid to the vehicles soon came home to roost, and the unreliability that ensued was addressed by London & Country taking over the services and running them from Addlestone. Apparently new engines were then fitted to the buses, which may have had more of an effect on reliability than simply changing garages.

In 1993 Steve and Christine Telling decided to buy back the business from Drawlane, with help from Julian Peddle, who had made a name for himself with Stevensons of Uttoxeter and had interests in a number of independent bus/coach operators. In addition to the Byfleet coach business, which had a fleet of 25 coaches and still included the 606 bus route, Steve also acquired the Cardiff depot, though by then the coach business in Cardiff was no longer trading.

Five ex-Nottingham Atlanteans were bought to

Above: Tellings-Golden Miller's first foray into London Transport services was in Drawlane ownership when, as TGM Buses, it won the 116/117 between Staines and Hounslow. Elderly Leyland Nationals were used. This one, seen in Feltham, came from Midland Fox, TGM's parent company at the time. *C. J. Brown*

Left: Into buses big-time. Tellings-Golden Miller's first serious break into London bus services came with the 235 (Brentford–Sunbury Village), for which 14 new low-floor Plaxton-bodied Dennis Darts were bought. *Geoff Rixon*

Top right: TGM gradually expanded into the void left by Arriva in northwest Surrey; typical TGM buses in the area at the time were Mercedes Vario minibuses, though more Darts came later. *Geoff Rixon*

Right: With the Capital takeover came more London bus routes, including a batch of Optare Excels for the U3 (Heathrow–Uxbridge). The route was soon swapped with First, outside whose garage it terminated in Uxbridge, but the Excels were kept and moved to the 216 (Staines–Kingston), which had been run commercially by London United — but not commercially enough. Though largely outside London, it became an LT tendered route, and TGM won it. *Geoff Rixon*

run four school contracts in Cardiff, and on 20 September 1993 two cross-city services began, in competition with Cardiff Bus, between Ely and St Mellons/Pentwyn under the Cardiff Bluebird name. Eventually Cardiff Bluebird became a serious competitor in Cardiff, with a fleet of 40 vehicles for a peak vehicle requirement of 34, running over most routes in the city, undercutting Cardiff Bus's fares and offering passengers change, as an alternative to Cardiff Bus's farebox policy. Citing high fuel costs, TGM pulled out of Cardiff on 7 September 1996 and sold its fleet to its competitor.

Back in Surrey, Tellings-Golden Miller had become purely a coach operator — but for less than a month. In March 1995 that Volvo/Caetano bus was sold along with the 606 service to London & Country, but on 25 March TGM started a significant new operation. For the first time in Steve Telling's ownership the company had won a London Transport contract, for the S3 service from Sutton to Worcester Park, and three Mercedes 709D minibuses with Plaxton bodywork were bought. Carrying distinctive registration numbers (M70, 80, 90 TGM), these were to be the first of many Mercedes minibuses and operated the first of many London services. London's tendering regime had moved on since the days of the 116/117; no longer was lowest cost everything, and from the S3 onwards Tellings-Golden Miller was able to operate new vehicles on London services — no longer would reliability be a problem.

During 1997 TGM won its first major London bus route — the 235 from Sunbury to Brentford — from London United. The 235 had been formed by the splitting of the 237, and London United held the contracts for both halves. However, the other section, still numbered 237, from Hounslow to Shepherds Bush, was also lost to another growing independent in southwest London — Armchair Passenger Transport. The 235 needed 12 buses, and 14 low-floor Dennis Darts were acquired to run it from the following January.

There was to be no turning back. TGM was entering the big time as a bus operator. Towards the end of 1998 Arriva, as successor to London & Country, was cutting back its services in Surrey. Driver shortages were the official reason, although it was an area where it was virtually impossible to generate the sort of profits demanded by a big PLC. Already TGM was picking up Surrey services through the tendering system; the first was the 513 between Kingston and Cobham, followed by the 512 and 514 in the same area. In a twist of irony TGM also gained the 564, a little service from Whiteley Village, near Hersham, to Walton-on-Thames. The irony of this was that the trunk of this service was the old 264, which Ben Stanley had taken over from London Transport more than 20 years earlier; Tellings might have ended up running it very much earlier had it achieved its goal of buying Ben Stanley.

In December 1998 Arriva withdrew from service 471 (Kingston–Woking), and this passed to TGM; then, the following May, as Arriva prepared to close its Leatherhead garage, another London Transport service, the 465 between Teddington and Dorking, came TGM's way, and seven recent Dennis Darts, still in London & Country livery, were leased to the company to run it. However, there was to be bigger expansion into London tendered routes in May 1999, when TGM took over Capital Logistics, a growing coach and bus operator based primarily at Heathrow but also with some operations at Gatwick. This brought a large site at Sipson Road, just to the north of Heathrow.

As well as being a major coach operator and running a substantial airside operation at Heathrow, Capital had latterly gained some London bus routes; these included the U3 from Heathrow to Uxbridge, which had become quite a high-profile operation through its use of upmarket Optare Excels featuring double-glazing and air conditioning. The U3 terminated right outside First CentreWest's garage in Uxbridge, and it made sense to swap the U3 for First CentreWest's 490 route between Hatton Cross and Richmond, which had made more sense to First when it still had its London Buslines operations (acquired from Len Wright) but was now rather out on a limb. The Optare Excels were kept and used on the 216 (Kingston–Staines), which TGM had won from London United.

More high-profile, for all the wrong reasons, was route 60 (Old Coulsdon–Streatham), one of the first in London to have low-floor double-deckers, but one on which just about everything that could go wrong did go wrong. Amongst its other difficulties, Steve Telling was appalled at the problems of vandalism on certain sections of the route, and the brand-new DAF double-deckers, built to a high standard, were in a terrible state as a result. They weren't to last long here; on 4 March 2000 TGM managed to dispose of route 60 and its double-deckers — apart from the Cardiff operation, the only double-deckers ever run by the company — to Arriva London South. Ironically this was the operator which had lost the route in the first place. The 60 had been run from a site in Croydon, and the opportunity was taken at the same time to dispose of the other route in that quarter of London, the S3, which passed to Epsom Buses.

Other routes gained with Capital Logistics were Hounslow local services H24 and H26 and one of the last vestiges of the old Green Line network, the 726, which by now ran from Heathrow to Bromley using unusual coach-seated Ikarus-bodied DAF SB220s. Both H26 and 726 were retained through the tendering system, and new Alexander ALX300-bodied Volvo B10BLEs were bought for the 726, which have been particularly successful vehicles for the operator. They are amongst the very few 12m single-deckers on any London service.

Soon after Capital Logistics was acquired, Tellings-Golden Miller's commitment to London services was to grow again. Arriva was now trying to offload its small depot in Hounslow, which had been set up to run two local London Transport services, H21 and H28, which TGM took over from 3 July 1999, bringing yet more London & Country green buses to the fleet, including six Mercedes minibuses and seven East Lancs EL2000-bodied Dennis Darts.

Tellings-Golden Miller was in need of extra premises for its growing network and had opened negotiations with London Transport to lease part of Fulwell garage. The old tram depot at Fulwell, near Twickenham, lay at an angle between two major roads and had an entrance at either end. After privatisation it had been split into two, with London United occupying one half of it, with its entrance into Wellington Road, and the other half lying vacant. Fulwell is a very old shed, built in 1903 for London United Tramways, and in May 1931 had become London's first trolleybus depot. Still with its old cobbles and tram track in place, and with a gantry for lifting tram bodies from their trucks, Fulwell has a preservation order on it, rather restricting LT's ability to dispose of it; in the interests of maintaining scope for competition for route contracts, LT had not been prepared to allow London United to occupy both ends of the site, despite that operator's acute shortage of space.

Fulwell seemed an ideal site from which to operate TGM's services, but it suddenly became unnecessary with the acquisition of the big site in Sipson Road. However, in April 2000 the Capital Logistics coach and airside operation was sold, to Airlinks (by now a National Express subsidiary), which was rapidly increasing its presence at both Heathrow and Gatwick airports, both as a coach operator and as a contractor to BAA, and again TGM was faced with needing to find space for its growing fleet. Negotiations over Fulwell were reopened with LT, and on 15 April 2000 TGM's new head office became The Old Tram Depot, Stanley Road, Twickenham. The coach fleet, now more than

40 strong, and 80 vehicles for London services were moved into Fulwell, 'which', said the company at the time, 'gives us significant scope for further growth'. It did, but by the beginning of 2003 the site was full, and consideration was being given to moving the coach fleet to a new site to allow for further expansion of the bus fleet. Not that sites suitable for running a quality fleet of 40 coaches are ten-a-penny in West London.

The front of the new depot was rebuilt imaginatively to create office space, while inside are impressive maintenance facilities and a paint bay. Those cobbles and tram lines were covered over with tarmac to create a suitable parking area for the bus and coach fleet, but before the allegations of sacrilege start flying, this was done carefully to preserve the original features below the surface. Sadly cobbles and tramtracks are not entirely compatible with Health & Safety requirements in a modern bus-parking area.

The fleet used for Surrey bus services remained at Byfleet, and this too was to grow. Arriva's continuing retrenchment brought more growth: the 441 from Heathrow to Englefield Green became a TGM service and received funding from Heathrow's owner BAA to improve frequency and extend the operating day. Further withdrawals by Arriva were filled by operators such as White Rose, which was to go out of business in early 2002. More Surrey services were taken over as a result, and a selection of Dennis Darts was rented to cover them, until in September 2002 the network was revised and tendered by Surrey County Council. TGM won the five-year tenders on the basis of running new buses on them, and 12 Dart SLFs recently taken out of service by Armchair were hired to run them, in Armchair livery, until 11 new Dennis Dart MPDs arrived in January 2003. By this time more new Darts were arriving, as the 235 and 465 were won again for another term. In line with Transport for London's requirements for buses on its services to be 80% red, Tellings-Golden Miller's distinctive livery of white, yellow and blue was modified with red replacing most of the white on batches of new Darts with both Plaxton Pointer and Caetano Nimbus bodywork. There was further expansion in Surrey in June, when routes 555/556/557 (Heathrow–Walton-on-Thames/Addlestone) were won from London United, although the 10 additional MPDs used thereon are based at Twickenham.

Today Tellings-Golden Miller, from its humble origins of picking up the pieces between LT's red and green buses, is now the dominant operator in the border area between southwest London and northwest Surrey. It is thus able to offer very useful

Above: An unusual legacy from Capital was the old Green Line 726 from Heathrow to Bromley, as it had become. When it was re-tendered TGM retained it and introduced new Alexander ALX300-bodied Volvo B10BLEs — a type unique on a London bus service. *Geoff Rixon*

Below: TGM's later Darts are dual-door buses, as required for all London bus services other than those run by smaller buses. They are also dual-sourced, with bodywork from Plaxton and, as in this case, Caetano, with its Waterlooville-built Nimbus. *Geoff Rixon*

Above: **London operations now require buses to be 80% red, which TGM has interpreted fairly literally, by covering 80% of its livery with red paint. One of the first was this Plaxton-bodied Dart SLF, at Hampton Court on the R68 from Richmond.** *Geoff Rixon*

Left: **Consolidation in northwest Surrey meant that a whole raft of services which had been operated commercially — or semi-commercially — by Arriva and a motley collection of successors were put out to tender, and TGM won the bulk of them. Buses were needed in a hurry, and while new vehicles were in build a batch of low-floor Darts just replaced on one of neighbouring rival Armchair's London contracts was rented. They were smartly turned out in Armchair livery, with Tellings-Golden Miller fleetnames.** *Geoff Rixon*

network benefits in the area and has brought a welcome stability to services on the Surrey side of the border after several years of uncertainty and service reductions. The buses running from Byfleet now operate on 15 Surrey services, including many which have their origins in London Transport routes, mainly green ones such as the 441, 451 and 461, plus the 515 (Kingston–Guildford) and associated routes which have their origins in Green Line service 715. The 218 is more familiar as one of the two routes which saw the end of red RFs, the other, the 216, also being a TGM route but now an LT tendered service and home to those ex-Capital Optare Excels; both link Kingston with Staines, running along opposite sides of the Thames.
In addition, Byfleet runs the Kingston University services and a number of school services. In January 2003 the Surrey fleet comprised 28 Dennis Dart SLFs, two Northern Counties-bodied step-entrance Darts (used mainly for driver training) and 22 Mercedes minibuses, including 10 Varios.

In addition to the coach fleet, Twickenham runs 14 Transport for London services, including the 216, 235, 465, 490 and 726 already mentioned, plus the 203 (Hounslow–Staines) and various H- and R-numbered routes in Hounslow and Richmond.
In January 2003, with the exception of the seven Volvo B10BLEs and eight Optare Excels, all were

run by 95 Dennis Dart SLFs, including 36 with Caetano Nimbus bodywork; the rest have the more usual Plaxton Pointer. However, that figure was inflated slightly by the fact that the oldest buses in the London fleet — 14 R-registered Dart SLFs — were being replaced on the 235 by new Caetano Nimbus examples; most were due to be refurbished and painted in a dedicated livery for Surrey route 441.

There is also a third Tellings-Golden Miller depot, in Portsmouth. This is Excelsior's former depot there, which was bought from Excelsior's owner, Flights, when the Excelsior business went into receivership, though TGM took over no vehicles. It did, however, take over Excelsior's National Express commitment from Portsmouth and runs 11 coaches from it, though they come to Fulwell for

Below and right: **Progress down the years. In February 1968 Golden Miller was the 'little guy' in the area (unlike the Big Guy concrete mixer just visible in the background). The ex-Northern General Albion Aberdonian sets down at Shepperton on the 602. Almost exactly 35 years later, a new Dart picks up at the same stop on what in 1968 was Shepperton's main bus route, the 218 (Staines–Kingston). Smart new Surrey County Council bus stops had recently been erected; LT flags had not been seen in the area for many years. The fence by the bus stop had also not long been replaced, no doubt having been weakened by the bulk of the author leaning against it while waiting many an hour for a bus there.** *Passenger Transport; Stephen Morris*

maintenance. The company is also the majority shareholder in Linkline of Harlesden, which had also been acquired by Drawlane and was bought back from British Bus.

There are, incidentally, two Tellings-Golden Miller companies. Logically one might think that the London operations from Fulwell and the Surrey operations from Byfleet are two different operations, but this is not the case. The two companies are separate bus and coach operations, and although some head-office functions are common to both, the coach company is managed completely separately. Coach and bus operations may share certain engineering disciplines but have little else in common, and few businesses that try to combine bus and coach operations do so successfully. Although the bus and coach companies will help each other out, and a bus driver may drive a coach when there is particularly high demand, the fact that both prosper is down to the fact that they are kept so separate.

Not often realised is that the Status Group, set up by Steve Telling and Julian Peddle to bring together a number of smaller operators throughout the country, covers only the coach company. Messrs Telling and Peddle have between them a shareholding in each of the Status companies, though in practice it is not a group in the sense of a Stagecoach or a Blazefield; rather, it gives the constituent companies economies of scale and greater buying power, and handles things like insurance and tyre contracts rather than anything more fundamental to the businesses, which retain their autonomy and individual ownership.

From a Bedford OB bought in 1955 by F. G. Wilder and a Bedford VAM bought in 1972 by Steve Telling, via a fascinating but small-scale bus operation from the 1960s, has grown one of the major names in the bus scene in London and its surroundings. Tellings-Golden Miller now provides employment for well over 500 people, and its smart buses in white, blue and yellow — and increasingly, in the case of the Fulwell fleet, with a large area of red — now dominate the area.

AN ABSENCE OF
ATLANTEANS

You don't know what you've got till it's gone, says *Peter Rowlands* as he looks back on a Newcastle adolescence ... and sometimes you can't see it even when it's there.

You could call it a wail, or a scream, or a roar. All I knew was that it was loud and it was wrong. This was not how to drive a bus.

It was the sound of Leyland Atlanteans being driven far too fast in the wrong gear, and it came from the stretch of road behind the house where I grew up in the leafy suburb of Gosforth, just outside Newcastle-upon-Tyne.

To be more precise, the road was actually beyond another row of houses that backed on to ours, so I couldn't actually see the offending Atlanteans (or should I say offended Atlanteans?). I could only hear them. Visually, they were conspicuous by their absence.

Over the years I would sometimes crane fruitlessly from the top-floor window to catch the merest glimpse of the road and those yellow buses

on it. Not a chance. All I could see was well-manicured gardens and neat upmarket semi-detached houses.

The road in question was Kenton Road, and this was the stretch between the Salters Road junction and 'the roundabout' (the only one in the whole vicinity). Town-bound, it represented a steady gradient about a third of a mile long, and as it was purely residential there were few passengers and fewer bus stops. So bus drivers on service 27 could let rip if they were so inclined.

A lot of them evidently were. But they couldn't get far before they had to start slowing for the roundabout, so a lot of them would simply flick the gear lever down into third. The revs would shoot up and the Leyland 600 engine would scream. Being at the front of the vehicle while the engine was at the back, the driver was probably less aware of the sound he was producing than bystanders in the street.

What a beguiling gearchange! Such a simple little electric box, so readily able to make bad drivers of even the best. If early Atlantean engines were sometimes prone to overheating, you have to wonder how much blame the drivers had to take.

Leyland called the system Pneumocyclic. It said so on the gearchange unit. I always assumed the name had the same pronunciation as in 'cyclical', but then in later years, I found out it was pronounced as in 'cycle', so there you go.

Whatever it was, I later found it was an electronic control linked to an air-operated actuator on the rear-mounted epicyclic gearbox. That unit, in turn, had its heritage in the old Wilson preselector gearboxes of the 'Thirties and 'Forties, latterly produced by Self-Changing Gears (the company founded by Irish-born engineer Walter Gordon Wilson, who developed the system).

Not that I thought all this through when the first Atlanteans appeared in Newcastle in 1960. Still, I was fascinated by the apparent simplicity of the new system. The driver just clicked the lever into the next gear; he didn't even need to take his foot off the throttle.

The trouble was, it simply didn't seem to occur to a lot of drivers that they weren't actually banned from doing so. Those that did were able to produce beautifully smooth, lurch-free rides. Those that didn't could have you lunging for the nearest handhold throughout the journey. I remember once watching a good driver all the way from Gosforth to 'town' via Grandstand Road, and marvelling at the discovery that you didn't have to fling your passengers around if you chose not to.

Some years later, at the end of the 1960s, I had a rather different but equally unsettling journey into town – my last journey, it turned out, on a much older bus that had always been my favourite type: one of Newcastle Transport's 1950 batch of open-platform AEC Regent IIIs with Northern Coachbuilders bodywork. The young driver, who apparently had a grudge against the world, and especially against this particular bus, drove it as if its very existence was a personal affront to him, thrashing it up to maximum revs in every gear, and standing on the brakes at every traffic light.

The journey from Gosforth involved two long stretches with virtually no stops: at least half a mile along Grandstand Road, and then a good mile along the Great North Road — two sides of the famous Town Moor. So the bus had no escape from the driver's ire. On alighting in the city centre, I felt like offering it a private apology for his heavy-footed insouciance, but I don't suppose it would have taken a lot of notice, being an inanimate object and so on.

It was rather an undignified swansong, though, for 20 years of sterling service. These were the buses that bore me to my first school, and whose tuneful combination of AEC engine and constant-mesh gearbox provided such a cheerful accompaniment to my early adolescence.

To be strictly accurate, I could only catch an AEC to school if I had the energy to arrive at my stop by 7.25 in the morning to catch the early service 30. If I missed that, the next was the 24, which was run by Park Royal-bodied Guy Arabs of Gateshead & District. These were characterised by their rather

Above left: **Atlanteans were still roaring down Kenton Road in 1995, when this Alexander-bodied AN68 was photographed at the top of the incline, just after passing the Salters Road junction.** *Peter Rowlands*

Right: **In 1995 some buses reached Gosforth by a more circuitous route than in the 1960s, passing the General Hospital at Fenham. This one is seen arriving at the Haymarket junction in Newcastle's city centre.** *Peter Rowlands*

sombre dark maroon livery and tuneless Gardner engine, and by the sense of foreboding they engendered.

The fact that yellow and maroon buses inter-worked is intriguing in itself now, although at the time it was just another piece of information to assimilate and accept. On town-bound journeys, all buses seemed to be bound for exotic-sounding places like Low Fell (on the south side of Gateshead). This free and easy movement of buses between the two big centres continued right up to the time the Metro system opened at the end of the 'Seventies; then routes were changed radically, and cross-river services were mostly withdrawn in a bid to drive passengers on to the new trains.

Something else I didn't know in my early school days was that those maroon buses were among the first ever operated by Gateshead & District, which itself was a new company in the form it then took. Until 1950 it had been purely a tram operator — not that I ever saw any evidence, sadly, apart from the tantalising hint of tram tracks still visible around

Newcastle's Central station in the early 'Fifties.

Another thing I didn't know was that the bodies of those 1950 Regents had been built scarcely half a mile from the city centre by Northern Coachbuilders, whose factory was on another side of the Town Moor, in Claremont Road. What's more, that batch of 30 bodies was one of the last ever produced there. Subsequently, the company was

subsumed into Smith's Electric Vehicles, a company started by the same Smith family behind the region's famous Rington's tea. Bus building in Newcastle came to an abrupt end before I even knew it had started.

In any case, how is a young person supposed to understand the difference between chassis maker and bodybuilder? That puzzle nagged at me for many years. I clearly remember the name 'Northern Coachbuilders' displayed inside those buses, but what did coachbuilding actually mean? After all, the bus was an AEC Regent; it said so on the front.

I was also puzzled by the fact that superficially similar-looking Bristol buses were to be found down on Gosforth High Street in the red livery of United Automobile Services. (These were Ks and KSWs, I later found.) How could this be?

Only later did I discover that the squarish NCB body was actually a blatant copy of an Eastern Coach Works design whose origins could be traced right back to the wartime years. NCB widened it from the previous 7ft 6in to 8ft, but otherwise the design debt was unmistakable. The same design was also built on Guy chassis for the Northern General group, and some actually went to Gateshead & District, though I only ever saw one of these once on a rare trip south of the river.

By the same token, I had to acknowledge the existence of other AEC Regents in the Newcastle fleet with quite different bodies by NCB and

Massey. How could one model have multiple identities like this? They rubbed shoulders with seemingly ancient Daimlers and all-Leyland Titan PD2s, which happily matched some operated by Gateshead.

I still had the same sense of confusion when Newcastle rolled out its Atlanteans. The first ones I saw had Metro-Cammell-Weymann bodies, and to me that defined the 'proper' appearance of an Atlantean. But then quickly they were joined by different-looking versions with bodies by Alexander. By this time it was dawning on me that 'bodybuilding' meant something more than just trim.

I also didn't know then that Alexander would build relatively few of those early flat-fronted Atlanteans' bodies, or that, apart from Newcastle, Northern General and its subsidiaries were the main customers. At the time, Alexander was really just limbering up for the launch of its enduring A-type body, with curvy front end and swept-round windscreens. The tables were turned when this appeared; MCW soon followed suit with a body that many regarded as basically a copy.

I'd have to dissent; the back end was pure MCW, and at the admittedly similar front, a vent inset into

The author's all-time favourite buses were AEC Regents from 1950, with locally-built Northern Coachbuilders bodywork that was essentially a copy of contemporary ECW designs.
R. H. G. Simpson

Right: **Northern Coachbuilders'
narrow 1948 bodies had the
company's own hallmark style,
slightly reminiscent of contemporary
Weymann buses. This Regent
is bound for Spital Tongues, where
the factory was located.**
R. H. G. Simpson

Below: **The definitive Atlantean
body style? This is how Newcastle's
early PDR1 models looked with
their MCW bodies, although the
very first ones had only single
headlamps.** *R. H. G. Simpson*

the curved dome somehow managed to make the MCW body look quite different from the equivalent Alexander. I always preferred the MCW version — yet another occasion when, perversely, I latched on to a copy and preferred it to the original.

By the early 1970s, when the sound of screaming Atlanteans on Kenton Road had become an established fact of local life, the earlier PDR1 models were being joined by the replacement AN68 version, with later Alexander AL-type bodywork, bigger Leyland 680 engine and (slightly) better sound insulation. These were the buses that survived right into the Stagecoach era of the 1990s,

by which time Atlanteans had been running in the yellow livery of Newcastle and then Tyne & Wear for more than 35 years.

Over those years I learned a lot about the bus industry that I couldn't have known as a child. It's the experience we all go through — making sense of what we see, and reconciling facts that seem illogical. And as we understand how things are, we can see better how they could be improved.

I was glad when Atlanteans began to replace older vehicles; they offered so many obvious benefits, especially for passengers. And I'm even more glad that they've been supplanted in turn by far quieter, smoother-riding low-floor models. That's progress.

But I was also sad when the last front-engined buses disappeared from Newcastle at the turn of the 'Seventies. The status quo you are born to is emblazoned in your mind with an intensity that nothing else can match. Likewise I was sorry when Stagecoach finally started pulling Atlanteans out of Newcastle in the mid-'Nineties (and dropped the yellow livery they'd worn as well). Peace reigns in Kenton Road at last, but it's a Pyrrhic victory in some ways.

Happily, Atlanteans are being preserved, and one of those 1950 Regents also survives under the auspices of the North East Bus Preservation Society. It returned to the show circuit after a long absence in 2000. Whether it's the one that was thrashed so remorselessly that day in the late 1960s I'll never know, but I'd like to think it might be.

Left: **Few operators apart from Newcastle and Gateshead & District featured Alexander's first attempt at Atlantean bodywork, with its flat front and back and curved dome.** *R. H. G. Simpson*

Below: **This is Gateshead & District's take on the early Alexander Atlantean, but in the later green livery. Only single headlamps here.** *R. H. G. Simpson*

Right: **After a restrained start, Alexander came out with a flamboyant swept-round front end for later bodies on PDR1 Atlantean chassis. This one is seen in front of the Central station before it was sandblasted in the 1960s.** *R. H. G. Simpson*

Below right: **Although MCW clearly copied Alexander's swept-round Atlantean body style, its version was subtly different — something that the vent in the roof dome emphatically underlined.** *R. H. G. Simpson*

ROUND THE BEND

Robert E. Jowitt, in his usual articulate vein, meditates over four decades on the career of the articulated bus abroad and latterly in Britain, coming down as might be expected in favour of the former …

All photographs by Robert E. Jowitt, except where sta

The first time I ever came across this particular monstrosity was, so far as I can recall, through a photograph in the pages of the *Daily Telegraph* or some such other erudite organ in the mid-1950s, the example in question being an articulated trolleybus in the streets of Moscow. So, well, with this being the height of the Cold War and all that history you wouldn't especially believe anything about Muscovite achievements, would you, even be they recorded in such respectable pages. Such monstrosities bore no possible resemblance to buses as the British knew them, and anybody who read John Wyndham was well aware you must never believe in myths coming from those parts …

Only then, a couple of years later, in my first forays into what is known in old folk-songs as

High-Germanee, I discovered that these unlikely monsters actually existed; and, while remaining faithful to the trams and railways which from the start I had loved so much better, I could not deny the charms of this outrageously fantastic variant of the bus scene.

I cannot now recall, 45 years later, which among two first caught my fancy. But suffice it to say it was either the Deutsche Bundespost buses working on quasi-rural services out of Paderborn, Westfalen, or else, variously, trolleybuses and buses, and variously on three or four axles, engaged on urban service in Dortmund … and, in other words, I had found true-life examples just like the Moscow mammoth legends.

Over the next decade, all through the swinging 'Sixties, I encountered plenty more. Mostly they were trolleybuses, generally they were in Germany or Switzerland, some of them were in Austria or Italy, usually they were on three axles with the third taking charge of the swinging bit at the back, but in Milano in Italy they were a bit more fanciful.

I suppose that at this point I must attempt to be a bit more technical — though regular readers of my words will know that I fall in love with buses or trolleybuses for their outward artistic virtues as decorations of the street scene rather than for whatever the make or rarity or otherwise may be — and so I will try to throw in a few helpful if possibly

Left: **With a rump nearly as elegant as a 1930s saloon car this 1950s MAN, in Dortmund, Germany, in 1959 clearly depicts the period German espousal of double rear axles on the back end of an articulated bus, copied on buses elsewhere in Germany.**

Below: **Spread over half a dozen German operations in trolleybus form (30 examples) and elsewhere with identical bodywork in diesel form was the 1961/2 Henschell offering. This example is one sold over the border, to Salzburg, Austria, seen in the spring of 1964 with an almost Edinburgh-like backdrop of the Schloß.**

inaccurate descriptions. So far as I can make out, most German articulated trolleybuses had an oval frontispiece which marked them as Henschel, a well-known German commercial-vehicle builder, and I suspect that most of the articulated motor buses came from Büssing or MAN … of which the same may be said.

Straying over the border into Salzburg, Austria, I encountered some more Henschel articulated trolleybuses, identical to various German examples, running about with thoroughly Austrian-looking articulateds by Gräf & Stift, celebrated producer of Austrian PSVs. I met further examples of these latter products in Linz and Leoben; and all of these specimens, if disgustingly new and fresh from the factory, were an inspiring token of faith in trolleybus solidarity.

Swiss examples, if equally a sign of belief in trolleybus superiority, were less readily identifiable, and perhaps it will suffice here to say, rather than delving into a lot of unpronounceable Swiss trade names, that they were all, inside and out, entirely and Swissly indigenous.

As for the Italian lot, either trolleybus or motor bus, I was brought up to believe that every vehicle

Left: In the early 1960s the local manufacturer Gräf & Stift bulked fairly large on the Austrian articulated trolleybus scene with numerous examples in Salzburg and Linz and this one, in Leoben. The triangle on the roof denotes that a trailer was being hauled (common practice then on Austrian commercials) and affects the contemporary (then) viewpoint on articulated buses.

Below: If not the cat among the pigeons ... This Büssing articulated is on urban service in Frankfurt, Germany, in 1964, thoroughly Teutonic in period style.

Above right: Spaghetti ... or the almost unique 1-2-1 wheel arrangement as applied to 90 Milano Fiat 2472F articulated trolleybuses supplied between 1958 and 1965, seen here in 1969.

Far right With two lads raising the dust on the left we see here the Torino-Rivoli inter-urban service, attended by both articulated diesels and trolleybuses, in bodywork almost identical, with in this 1966 view a Fiat diesel alleged to carry 150 passengers.

apparently the population of Lyon shared with me my antipathy towards these obscenities as uncomfortable or over-crowded or rough-riding or any of the other complaints generally laid at the latest issue of new buses. And they may not really have been all that bad, but, whatever the case, their career on the streets of Lyon was relatively short, namely 12 years.

Apart from Lyon the French were perhaps slow into getting onto the scene of articulated buses, even if they were so fast in scrapping trolleybuses that they never at all entered the scene of articulated trolleybuses … except for an incredibly daring 1950 prototype — a Spaghetti four-axle Vetra VA4 based on the classic VA3 which was tried briefly in Paris and then exiled to Algeria — but once the Lyon Berliet disaster had been forgotten the French took the new style to their hearts and their streets. The Berliet PR180, notable for having

on the roads of Italy was a Fiat (except when it was an Alfa Romeo which, as I then understood the case, was far too sporting to enter into the public-service-vehicle category, though I have since learned that Alfa Romeo indeed dabbled in trolleybuses, or else an Om which seems to have been restricted to the realms of heavy goods vehicles), so I assumed, even if mistakenly, that all those lovely articulated trolleybuses in Milano and those equally lovely articulated trolleybuses which came on an inter-urban route into Torino from Rivoli were all Fiats. Anyway, even if they weren't — and who really cares? — they had their charms, and the principal charm about some of the Milano specimens was that while the articulated back-end of the trolleybus was on a single axle the front half of the trolleybus claimed the almost unknown rarity in such situation of twin rear axles. If trolleybuses were given wheel-arrangement notations like railway locomotives are — such as Mikado or Mountain, Pacific or Atlantic — would this be a candidate for Spaghetti?

Regardless, however, of what I have said above, and much as I admired the examples mentioned, more particularly certainly in trolleybus form but with much acceptance of the diesel alternative, I must herewith state that there was one set of articulated buses which I could in no way tolerate. This was in Lyon, where from 1966 some decidedly dreadful Berliet PH12-180s effected major inroads into the scrapping of a trolleybus system — the greatest in France — which a few years previously I had utterly adored. These Berliets … these things … were so horrible that I could not bring myself to photograph them … much though I regret this now … but

its engine at the very back, first appeared in Paris in the early 1980s, and a list of the locations of French artics now would appear almost — if not quite — like an index from the Michelin guidebook.

So then the habit spread further west, to be picked up in Iberian places such as Bilbao or Vigo, where either they had or they might have had, according to history, useful fleets of second-hand London 'Q1' trolleybuses operating, and even into Portugal, where they had the most wonderful tramway systems in the world. Lest the above remark may be obscure to any reader unacquainted with Spanish trolleybus history I must here add that Bilbao operated a number of second-hand London 'Q1' trolleybuses while Vigo kept several more in a shed but failed signally ever to operate them, and with this failure they were variously sold elsewhere — which has no part in this tale — or fell to pieces

Apart from examples beyond the Iron Curtain (and rare enough there) four-axle articulated trolleybuses were arch-rare, for apart from the Milano Spaghettis (and the experimental Vetra in similar style) there were only 10 1950 Alfa Romeos in Stockholm and a pair of c1955 Henschels starting in Neuss and passing on to Pforzheim, as seen here in 1963.

or were vandalised or broken up … but again this has no part in this tale, except to say that instead of 'Q1s' there were articulated buses in the streets of Vigo; and likewise in Bilbao when the 'Q1s' in that city succumbed to great old age and a Spanish political disinclination for electric vehicles in the streets.

And here again, on the subject of the replacing articulated diesels, I must profess some ignorance; I certainly thought they were pretty enough in their own twisty way, even if they were responsible — or not, as the case may be — for ousting Q1s from the highways, but as to what make they were I cannot give any opinion.

I am better informed about the streets of Porto, Portugal, where a host of beastly Volvo articulateds ousted my entirely beloved trams from the pavement-sides of the Praça Liberdade and several other choice locations as well. I knew they were Volvo because it said so in large letters on the front, and because I picked up somewhere — goodness knows where — a leaflet which described them in probably glowing, though to me incomprehensible, Portuguese terms and illustrated them in readily appreciable glowing colours including a picture of a scale model version.

Due to the inadequacies of the Jowitt filing system the said leaflet is not to hand, or in other words has got lost, but what is to hand is an actual sample, picked up in an Isle of Wight shop which deals in second-hand models of buses, of a Volvo articulated just like the one in the picture, now sitting on my bedside table. Underneath this model, with fairly badly collapsed front and rear axles (did this happen in real life, I wonder?) is simply the statement — along with a fairly decent interpretation of what the undercarriage might be — 'Volvo B10M' and the scale (1:50); no mention of Dinky Toys or later supplanters, so readers must assume, as I do, that the B10M designation is correct.

In these ramblings thus far I am straying, so far as Porto is concerned, into the mid-1980s and, in regard to that wretched bedside model, the late 1990s.

But all this was on foreign soil, with conceptions of public transport, even if quite sensible ones, floating over from somewhere beyond the Iron Curtain. We, in Great Britain, with our glorious tradition of double-deckers, did not need to learn about such foreign fantasies.

Then suddenly we did. And the first I heard of it was like this …

I have some repute as an operator of preserved Parisian buses of the 1930s and it was towards one of these specimens — probably c1980 on an 'Extravaganza Day', when said specimen was working a service alongside but in more-or-less accepted rivalry to the trams at the National Tramway Museum, Crich, Derbyshire — that a host of determined ladies, and possibly their husbands,

Right: **Spanish articulated buses (here an indigenous Pegaso in Bilbao, 1984) incorporated the Austrian-style warning triangle for 'trailer' built into the front canopy.**

Below: **One of the classic articulateds of the 1970s and 1980s was the Volvo B58/B10M, here in Portuguese form beneath Porto palms beside political graffiti.**

inspect the vehicle in question, which must have been engaged in exhibiting the serpentine charms of Continental transport to the Great British Public. Hindsight suggests it was probably an MAN. Sheffield, with new 'South Yorkshire' euphoria, indulged in several such buses, and followed them shortly afterwards with several Leyland-DABs, which looked like overgrown Nationals with tails.

I may add that I did not especially want to know, for as resident in Winchester — as I was then — what happened in Sheffield was almost as mythical as what happened in Moscow. But then, after a chequered second-hand career, as befell both the MANs and the Leylands, two of the latter turned up in Winchester, in the late 1980s, on Stagecoach (ex-Hants & Dorset) route 47 to Southampton, trying to cope with the several right-angle bends of our ancient city. One bus lasted only a few days in service, then was left rotting behind the bus station for some months to provide spares for the other; then both disappeared into oblivion … but I must say that while the second survived I made the most of riding the right-angles.

Then for more right-angles and more second-hand buses let us take a day trip to Dieppe in the mid-1990s, £10 for a family ticket and ten times as much again for family passport, food and drink. Now in my youth you caught a civilised packet-boat at Newhaven and disembarked from it straight onto a proper steam-hauled express on the quay which was effectively one of the streets of Dieppe. Nowadays the car-ferry terminal is on the opposite side of the harbour (to keep British motorists away from the streets?), so foot passengers are 'bussed' to where the railway has been dug up.

The bus, the highlight of the whole excursion, was a PR180, negotiating tighter-than-90° corners, attired outside in gaudily nautical livery but inside still flagrantly displaying its former Parisian fleet number.

from Sheffield, bore down sturdily with conversation approximately as follows:

Ladies: Where's this bus going?

Jowitt (as conductor): Up to the top end. 20 pence each.

Ladies: We don't have to pay. We gets free rides ont' trams.

Jowitt (politely, of course): This isn't a tram, although it may look like one, and could I perhaps ask what is your entitlement to free rides anyway?

Ladies: They said we could have free rides, 'cos we came here ont' Bendy-bus.

I do not recall how we resolved the argument, and I certainly was too busy with my own affairs to

Well, old French buses, like old soldiers, never die, or if they do they take a long time about it, but I thought that with the end of the Sheffield/ Winchester adventure the articulated habit had died in Britain.

Not so. In the later 1990s they were slinking in again. Or so I am told. I must admit I do not on the whole keep up with present-day bus developments — the former golden age being more to my taste —

but I suddenly encountered, as if to celebrate the new millennium, articulated buses in Birmingham with Travel West Midlands, then more with First in Southampton. Where had all the Atlanteans gone?

Upon enquiry among the *cognoscenti* — not about the Atlanteans but about the artics — I was informed I had missed out on Stagecoach motorway coaches of the mid-1990s — Volvo B10Ms, bodied by Plaxton or Jonckheere, apparently still swirling about today

Above: **An unidentified (possibly Heuliez) articulated getting the hump in Toulouse in 1989.**

Below: **The opposite of getting the hump is observed in Toulouse in the rain in 1989.**

Above: **Contrast in Nice, 1989, between (probably) Heuliez articulated and classic Saviem Standard SC10.**

Below: **In Birmingham in 2000 on this Travel West Midlands Mercedes-Benz the HGV-style 'long vehicle' notice employed on the rear of an earlier generation of English articulateds has given way to the informal 'Bendibus – the twice as long bus'.**

between Exeter and Plymouth — and a Mercedes registered K1 GRT with Grampian and thus then to First.

And more; for First is plainly into bendy-buses in a big way. Besides Southampton they have them — or have tried them (they appear to chuck them around a bit) — in Manchester, Leeds, Glasgow, London, Aberdeen and Bath. And in the last year or so Go-Ahead has installed Scanias in Gateshead and Mercedes Citaros with London General on the 507 and 521 — dozens, apparently — while Nottingham too has Scanias, and by the time these words appear in print Travel Coventry will have added more Citaros to the streets of that city.

I shall not dwell further on this progress. Those who want to know about it will know where to look. The charm of the articulated bus lay, for me, in the fact that it was utterly a Continental device.

Articulated buses within the shores of our little islands are to me, die-hard, nearly as alien as euros.

Let me add, as a kind of post-script, one sample of classic Continental articulation which I doubt we will ever see here, euros or not. In 1987 Paris introduced the Renault/Heuliez Megabus, a 24m-long three-section PR180-2 on four axles and 14 tyres and able to carry 200 passengers. Its bulk caused such frightful traffic jams that its career was brief, but in Bordeaux, where evidently bus lanes and such-like are better ordered, a fleet of a dozen or so similar vehicles operated all through the 1990s, and may be there now. I wasn't in Paris in 1987, and haven't been in Bordeaux since, but perhaps I ought to go there and chase them up. I should like to, if they are, though any photographic consequences would be far too late for this edition of *Buses Yearbook*.

And then one more myth, back beyond the Iron Curtain where we started. In Romania, in 1984, they brought out a three-section-articulated *five-axle* prototype trolleybus … but no; even though the Cold War is over, I am not going to hunt for that …

*Amidst the horrors of millennium urbanisation *spot the bus*! In typical Travel West Midlands surroundings a Mercedes-Benz bendibus can be distinguished above the second and third crosses of the upper row.*

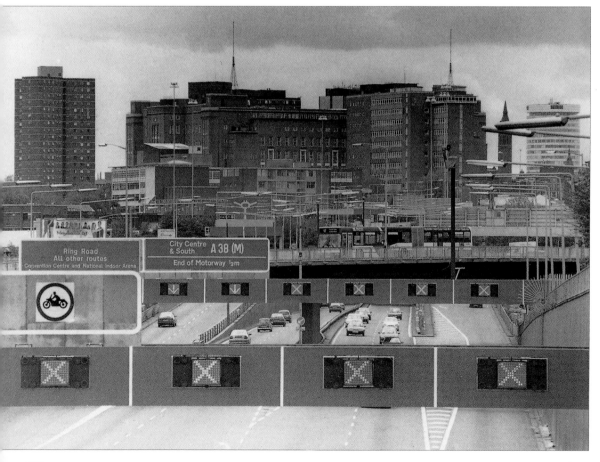

Above: By 1995 Sheffield was into a second generation of articulated buses — Danish-built Leyland-DABs — here spotted in the form of a Mainline-liveried bus at Meadowhall.
Malcolm Chase

Below: Arguably the greatest articulated bus of all, the French Megabus, with *three* sections, based on a PR180, suffered a brief and disastrous prototype career in Paris, but several examples went on to enjoy a successful and *lengthy* life in Bordeaux. Here is one outside the Gare St Jean in 1990.
Malcolm Chase

McKINDLESS
VARIETY

McKindless of Wishaw operates local services in the Wishaw/Hamilton area and also runs to Glasgow. *Billy Nicol* illustrates some of the variety to be found in the McKindless fleet.

Above: There have been many Leyland Nationals from a variety of sources. Among the more unusual is this 11.3m-long example which has been fitted with a Volvo engine and an Urban Bus front, which softens its appearance. It was new to South Wales Transport.

Left: In 1999 a Routemaster was added to the fleet and painted in the dark red and cream of Central SMT, for many years the major operator in the area. The standard McKindless livery is cream and green.

Top: More conventional double-deckers have included these ̶ormer National Bus Company vehicles. Nearer the camera is a 1975 Bristol VRT acquired from Southern Vectis in 1990 and

Above: Since 2000 the standard double-decker in the McKindless fleet has been the MCW Metrobus. Most have come from London; this is an ex-London United bus.

Above: Since 1999 second-hand Dennis Darts have figured strongly in the fleet. A 1990 Carlyle-bodied example loads in Hamilton. Like the Metrobus, it came from London United.

Below: Another ex-London United bus is this Dart with Plaxton Pointer body. Comprehensive route information is given on a board in the windscreen.

Top: Not all the McKindless Darts have come from London. This Wright-bodied bus, seen in central Glasgow, came from Go-Ahead Group in 2001.

Above: Big single-deckers include DAF SB220s with Optare Delta bodywork, purchased from Trent in 2001. McKindless is one of the very few Delta operators north of the border and runs Scotland's largest fleet of the type.

Right: The fleet also contains four examples of the Leyland Lynx – another type relatively rare in Scotland. This one, photographed in Wishaw in 2000, was new to Boro'line Maidstone in 1989.

TAKING THE

Roy Marshall took an interest in trolleybuses from an early age, as he recalls here.

TROLLEY

All photographs by the aut

Seen in Manchester city centre in 1948 is a 1946 Ashton Sunbeam W with Roe body to the relaxed utility specification which featured upholstered seats (instead of wooden slats) and extra opening windows. Behind is a prewar Manchester six-wheel Leyland. In the postwar years most of Ashton's operations were joint with Manchester.

Early in 1932 the municipal tramcars on our local service from Nottingham to Carlton had been replaced by trolleybuses — or 'railless', as they had become officially known locally. I was three at the time, but soon noticed the interior differences between the Park Royal bodies on the Karriers and those by Brush on the Ransomes. Thus began my love of the trolleybus. Two years later they were displaced by new Brush-bodied Karriers and Ransomes, and from 1942 each batch of utilities served this hilly route when new.

My interest in trolleybuses was heightened by spending family holidays in Southsea in 1937 and 1939, when I was introduced to the deep, comfortable, moquette-covered seating on the AEC four-wheelers of Portsmouth Corporation, which I considered far superior to the six-wheelers at home.

In September 1940 I started a 5½-year period of travelling each school day to a grammar school (known by the county council as secondary schools) situated near Bulwell depot. Surprisingly it was cheaper to make my cross-city journey by three trolleybuses rather than using two, as the half fare for a 1½d adult ticket was ½d, whereas that for a 2½d adult ticket was 1½d. The saving would be spent on fares into town on Saturdays, or to Trent Bridge to peer through the windows of the City

The first bulk order for trolleybuses in Belfast was placed with AEC, and 88 of these 664T models were delivered from 1941. Bodywork was by Harkness, a Belfast-based builder, using Park Royal frames.

Transport works to note repaints, body rebuilds or other developments. One of my journeys to or from school was often on a Notts & Derby vehicle — a four-wheel Weymann-bodied AEC, some of which were new early in the war and, from memory, included electric heating.

By this time I had visited relatives and travelled on trolleybuses in Derby and Huddersfield, and learned where other systems operated by reading *Modern Transport* and through library research. During school holidays, sometimes along with a friend, I made day trips by public transport to Manchester, Hull, Walsall, Wolverhampton, Birmingham and Rotherham, as well as to Bradford, St Helens and parts of the South Lancs system, from a holiday base in Elland, Yorkshire.

Visits to the remaining systems had to wait until I started work in 1946, when it became possible to visit Grimsby and Cleethorpes and to spend my annual week's holiday (yes, just one week) arranging tours by public transport to cover the other trolleybus systems.

During my travels I soon realised that systems differed not only in the make, type and livery of the vehicles but in the overhead fittings, layout and standard of maintenance which were most important to their smooth running. This is a subject which is, sadly, rarely mentioned. The overhead in Nottingham compared very favourably with that in neighbouring Derby.

As a schoolboy my ambition was to work for a trolleybus operator — ideally as a draughtsman, which would include designing overhead — but this was not to be until 1951, when I joined Nottingham City Transport in the traffic section. I soon discovered that the senior people in the section looked unfavourably upon the trolleybuses. They were route-bound, needed a separate group of drivers, and extensions into new housing estates were expensive. Their advantages of quietness, simplicity and use of locally produced electricity were ignored, and in 1958 I moved to a better post elsewhere and never again worked for a trolleybus operator, although by then I had the ambition to be a manager at one.

I did become a municipal manager, although not, alas, with trolleybuses.

Left: The highest-numbered trolleybus in the Birmingham fleet was 90, one of 12 Metro-Cammell-bodied Leylands of 1940. Twelve similar buses had also been delivered in 1937. Upon withdrawal in 1951 two of the bodies — including that of the bus shown here — were sold to Silcox of Pembroke Dock and fitted to new Bristol K6G bus chassis.

Below: Conversion to trolleybus of the Cardiff tram system began in 1941 but was delayed by the war. To convert the Docks routes, which ran under a low bridge, seven 1930 English Electric single-deckers were bought from nearby Pontypridd Uban District Council in 1947. They ran until 1950, being replaced by new BUTs.

Above: The small Cleethorpes system started in 1937 with the former tram service to Grimsby being run by trolleybuses in a joint operation with the latter town. The postwar Cleethorpes fleet included four BUT 9611Ts with Northern Coachbuilders bodies. Livery was grey and blue.

Below: In 1943/4 Darlington received 24 Karrier Ws with 32-seat Brush bodies. These replaced older trolleybuses in the fleet, including the last of the 1926 Strakers which had inaugurated trolleybus operation in the town.

Left: The Glasgow system did not start until 1949, the initial vehicles being BUT 9641Ts with London-style Metro-Cammell bodies; there were also some generally similar six-wheel Daimlers. The FYS registration series was used exclusively for Glasgow Corporation vehicles.

Below: In 1938/9 Huddersfield placed in service no fewer than 75 Karrier E6s with bodywork by Park Royal or Brush. This is a Park Royal-bodied bus and was basically a development of earlier deliveries. There was some similarity to Nottingham's trolleybuses; Huddersfield General Manager H. Godsmark had previously been Deputy General Manager at Nottingham. Note the three-piece front upper-deck window layout and the arrow-shaped direction indicators below the cab windows.

Right: This was the first of a new design of trolleybus for Hull, and it entered service in January 1953. The chassis was a Sunbeam MF2B, and the two-door body was by Roe. The intention was that they should be one-man-operated; they never were.

Centre right: As in Glasgow, Newcastle took trolleybuses with London-style bodywork by Metro-Cammell. These are two BUT 9614T models. The destination-indicator layout was inspired by that used in Huddersfield, the manager responsible having previously worked for the Yorkshire undertaking. The overhead wiring, incorporating support arms stretching across the road, was unusual.

Below: Two Brush-bodied Ransomes in Old Market Square, Nottingham, in 1948. The bus nearest the camera was new in 1934, the other in 1931. Both batches were prone to body movement, while the author recalls receiving an electric shock when boarding one of the 1931 vehicles on a wet day!

Above: Trolleybuses generally looked more modern than their motorbus equivalents, thanks to the smooth frontal profile of the body. Photographed in 1955, these two Portsmouth AEC 661Ts were the best part of 20 years old; dating from 1936/7, they were part of a batch of 76 which replaced most of the city's trams. Bodywork was by Cravens.

Below: Rotherham specified powerful 100hp motors on its centre-entrance single-deckers, to achieve high average service speeds. This is a 1937 Cravens-bodied AEC 664T, photographed in 1948, with some of its electrical gear mounted on the roof at the rear.

Top: To replace older vehicles, Southend purchased nine Sunbeam MF2s from Wolverhampton Corporation in 1950. New in 1937/8, these buses had 54-seat Park Royal bodies. The last trolleybuses to join the Southend fleet, they were withdrawn in 1953/4. Trolleybus operation ended in October 1954.

Above: In 1949/50 Wolverhampton bought 73 Park Royal-bodied Guy and Sunbeam trolleybuses. This is a Sunbeam MF2, seen in 1951.

Above: **A Hastings Tramways Sunbeam W with Weymann body loads in the town in the summer of 1952. It was new in 1948. Hastings Tramways was part of the BET group, and control of the operation passed eventually to sister company Maidstone & District, which in 1959 replaced the trolleybuses with Leyland Atlanteans.**

Right: **London Transport operated Britain's biggest trolleybus fleet and had over 1,000 in operation by 1940, the year this AEC 664T with body by the Birmingham Railway Carriage & Wagon Co entered service. The location is Aldgate.**